MW00560760

# Heavy Metal Rhythm Gu

Published by **www.fundamental-changes.com**

ISBN: 978-1-910403-24-2

Copyright © 2015 Rob Thorpe

Edited by Joseph Alexander

The moral right of this author has been asserted.

**www.fundamental-changes.com**

*Cover image copyright Shutterstock: Melis*

# Also by Fundamental Changes

# Contents

# Foreword

This book is a comprehensive guide for guitarists who wish to master the essential techniques and concepts in metal. It includes a wealth of material that is accessible yet challenging for beginner to intermediate guitarists.

Metal Rhythm Guitar examines the guitar playing at the roots of metal in the mid-1960s, such as Led Zeppelin and Deep Purple, and the New Wave of British Heavy Metal bands of the late '70s and early '80s like Judas Priest, Saxon and Iron Maiden. The thrash metal of bands like Metallica and Slayer will be studied, along with bands like Death, Pantera and Meshuggah who progressed the style and expanded the technical possibilities.

**Where did metal come from? Who were the first real heavy metal band?**

Fans and musicologists have suggested answers to both of these questions, but in my opinion, heavy metal was born in Birmingham, England in 1969 with the bell chimes, thunder, and the crashing guitar riff that opened Black Sabbath's first album.

Sabbath's guitarist, Tony Iommi, worked in the steel factories of industrial Birmingham, and the sounds of the machinery most likely influenced the ominous, dark rhythms of Black Sabbath's music. Black Sabbath's bassist, Geezer Butler wrote many of the band's lyrics. His interest in religion, fantasy, the occult and horror combined the lyrical subject matter with the industrial sounding music.

At that time, many bands had been moving in an increasingly heavy direction, but until now, the sound had remained planted in blues-rock. Black Sabbath introduced many of the ingredients that we now think of as essential characteristics of 'heavy metal', and for the first time The Blues took a back seat.

The next generation of rock musicians took the influence of Sabbath, Zeppelin, Mountain and other hard rock bands, distilling the heavier tone and darker lyrical subject matter and causing it to diverge further from rock and pop music trends.

While progressive rock explored unusual song forms and classical influences, the New Wave of British Heavy Metal (NWOBHM) bands like Judas Priest, Saxon and Iron Maiden created dramatic songs that balanced powerful instrumental music with the operatic vocal power of singers like Bruce Dickinson.

Meanwhile, musicians in San Francisco, California had been influenced by both the NWOBHM bands and the faster, more abrasive development of punk rock known as 'hardcore'. Hardcore punk exploded out of Southern California and across America in the late '70s, led by bands such as Black Flag. These musicians went on to develop thrash metal. Key figures were Dave Mustaine, James Hetfield, Jeff Hanneman and Scott Ian, who played in several notable bands before forming Metallica, Slayer and Anthrax.

Thrash metal also adopted the DIY ethic of indie record labels that characterised hardcore punk.

By the time these thrash metal bands came to record their standout albums such as *Master of Puppets* (Metallica, 1986) and *Rust in Peace* (Megadeth, 1990) their sound had become extremely polished and the complexity of compositions had developed greatly from their punk-influenced beginnings.

When thrash metal was adopted and progressed by a new generation 'death metal' was born, with important death metal scenes present in both Florida and Scandinavia. The ingredients of thrash metal (guttural singing, fast double kick drums, and intricate, technical guitar riffs) were all exaggerated in death metal music. Similarly, the bleak, lyrical subject matter developed into increasingly vivid depictions of graphic, satanic imagery.

At the same time, other bands were taking rock music in a new direction. Rather than exploring increasingly aggressive music, they built on the melodic and theatrical elements of bands like Iron Maiden. Power metal formed in the mid-'80s with European bands like Helloween, Blind Guardian and Stratovarius and was characterised by a more symphonic sound employing keyboards, vocal harmonies, orchestral elements and folk melodies to create rich textures. The lyrics frequently drew from pagan myths, or fantasy writers such as J.R.R Tolkien and H.P. Lovecraft.

Power metal's upbeat harmonies and melodic hooks were combined with the complexity and theatrical influence of the progressive bands like Yes and Rush to form progressive metal. This sub-genre raised the bar for virtuosity and featured technically demanding instrumental sections, strong vocal delivery, and complex song structures. Early pioneers included Fates Warning and Queensrÿche followed by Dream Theater and Symphony X.

No matter which sub-genre of metal you connect with, the following journey through the development of metal guitar playing will help you to understand the music and play it authentically. Understanding how the style evolved will help to turn you into a well-rounded and knowledgeable musician.

This book covers the key concepts and techniques common to *all* styles of metal and they can be applied however you wish. There is a logical progression from classic 'hard rock' through to more technically demanding modern metal ideas. Along the way we will cover all the relevant music theory including scales, rhythm and harmony, and how to apply these components to the guitar.

By the end of the book, you will have developed strong guitar technique and an understanding of the mechanics of metal guitar allowing you to write your own songs.

Have fun with these ideas but above all experiment and be creative with the information. Doing so will mean that you get the most out of this book and help you to grow rapidly as a musician.

Good luck, and have fun!

Rob Thorpe

You can download all the audio in this book for free from **www.fundamental-changes.com/download-audio.**

# Primer: Rhythm and Notation

Before we begin, it will be helpful to learn how to play and notate rhythms. This will help you to notate the music you write or transcribe, and also to practice efficiently.

**Note Values and Simple Time**

Musical notation combines information about both the pitch and duration of a note. Guitar tablature often misses rhythms off completely which can make the music hard to understand. Reading rhythmic notation will help you to understand how to play music without having to hear it first.

Western music is divided into *bars*, which show how the music is to be phrased. Bars are then further divided into individual *beats*. In most rock music there are four beats in each bar, and this is indicated by a *time signature* at the start of the sheet music.

Figure 1 shows two bars of **4/4** time. Each bar contains four 1/4 note beats. The numbers under the *stave* (musical notation) illustrate how to count through the bars. It may seem basic, but counting out loud when you play will help greatly later on when playing more complicated rhythms.

**Fig. 1:**

Some notes last longer than one beat. Figure 2 shows *whole notes* (four beats) and *1/2 notes* (2 beats).

**Fig. 2:**

Rhythmic notation is very logical because every note value is broken down into simple divisions of bars and beats. A time signature with a '4' on the bottom (like 4/4) means that each beat will always divide into multiples of two. The following example shows how each 1/4 note beat can be divided into 1/8th notes (two notes per beat) and 1/16th notes (four notes per beat).

Look at the counting under each stave. The basic 1, 2, 3, 4 pulse should remain at the same speed (tempo) while the shorter note values are squeezed in evenly into each beat. Each time we *subdivide* a note, we add another *tail* to the note's stem.

**Fig. 3:**

**Dotted Notes**

*Dotted notes* can also be used. Adding a dot next to the note head extends the length of a note by half its original value. The dotted 1/2 note in the following example lasts for three beats (1/2 + 1/4). This same concept applies to any note value.

In the second bar the dotted 1/4 notes last for three 1/8th notes each. (1/4 + 1/8)

**Fig. 4:**

**Rests**

As well as defining the length of each note that is played, we need a way to notate the space between notes when we require silence. This is the job of *rests* and every note has an equivalent rest value.

The symbols for rests are shown in figure 5.

**Fig. 5:**

Study the following figures to see combinations of note values that are likely to occur in real musical situations.

Clap, or strum a muted chord to play the following rhythms. They are included as audio examples so that you can hear them in context.

**Fig. 6a:**

**Fig. 6b:**

## Triplets and Compound Time

A triplet is simply three notes squeezed evenly into a single 1/4 note beat.

The following example shows a bar of 4/4 with triplets on beats two, three and four. Notice how they are counted.

**Fig. 7a:**

Triplets have a recognisable feel that will probably be familiar to you. You can hear them in Iron Maiden's *Phantom of the Opera* and Black Sabbath's *Black Sabbath* (4:35 onwards).

If triplets are used as the foundation of a piece of music, then a different time signature might be used to simplify the notation. *12/8* is an example of *compound time* and means that there are still four even beats in each bar, but now each beat has three divisions instead of two.

Figure 7b would sound the same as a bar of triplets in 4/4, but now the beats are naturally divided into threes. To account for this, each beat is actually a dotted 1/4 note, as shown by the metronome mark.

**Fig. 7b:**

There can be confusion about the difference between the time signatures of *3/4* and *6/8*, as they both contain a total of six 1/8 notes. The important difference is that each beat is divided differently.

In figure 8a, there are three even beats and each one is divided into two 1/8 notes.

In figure 8b, the *6/8* time signature is broken into two beats with each beat subdivided into three 1/8 notes.

**Fig. 8a:**

**Fig. 8b:**

Put simply, 3/4 has three strong pulses that are divided into two, while 6/8 has two strong pulses that are divided into three.

This primer covers the fundamentals of reading rhythmic notation. We'll cover other bits of notation as we progress, but this section forms the basis of everything that follows.

Don't worry if this is new to you, every example in this book can be heard on the accompanying audio examples. You can download them from **http://www.fundamental-changes.com/download-audio.**

# Chapter One: Roots of Metal

We will start by exploring the early blues-influenced styles of hard rock and heavy metal. The vocabulary found in the music of bands such as Deep Purple, Led Zeppelin, Cream, Black Sabbath and The Jimi Hendrix Experience set the blueprint for heavy metal's trajectory.

These bands had Rock 'n' Roll as an inspiration, but their '60s spirit of adventure and psychedelic experimentalism drew on folk, classical and jazz influences in their search for a new sound.

The first few musical examples show how the minor pentatonic scale is used in rock riffs. The five note minor pentatonic scale is the basis of most blues melodies, making it an essential sound, no matter what your taste in music.

First, we have a riff based around the E minor pentatonic scale, which is similar to ideas used by Jimmy Page and Richie Blackmore.

**Example 1a:**

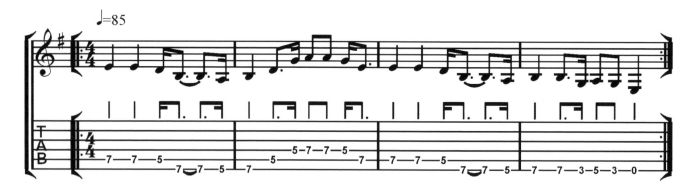

All the riffs in this book are brought to life by the way they are played so make sure to play them with plenty of attitude.

Try adding subtle grace notes, slides and vibrato to the examples in this book as I do on the audio example. It's these little details that can give simple musical phrases a lot of character.

In the next example, the 12/8 time signature means that each beat is split into three equal notes, a feel inherited from the blues origins of heavy metal. Listen to the audio and you'll hear the characteristic '**1&a 2&a**' groove.

**Example 1b:**

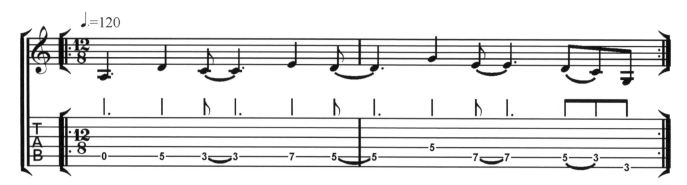

The next riff demonstrates a device called *anticipation,* which is a form of *syncopation* (playing between the beats). Pre-empting the beat gives forward motion and energy to the riff.

Compare the following example with the previous two, and try to notice why it sounds different. Compare music by Black Sabbath and AC/DC and you will hear that AC/DC uses a lot of anticipation whereas Sabbath's rhythms usually fall right on the beat.

**Example 1c:**

To play syncopated riffs accurately, keep your picking hand moving in a continuous down-up strumming motion, even when you're not actually playing the notes. Doing this helps you to keep in time with the pulse of the music.

Think of your picking hand as a mini conductor who keeps time for you, or as the needle on a record player so sound is only produced when your pick is in contact with the strings.

In the next example, double-stops are used to create a fatter sound. To get a bluesy feel and to help in achieving good vibrato, use the first or third fingers flattened across the fretboard to play each double-stop.

Many classic riffs by bands like Deep Purple and Led Zeppelin use double-stops (such as the ubiquitous *Smoke on the Water).*

**Example 1d:**

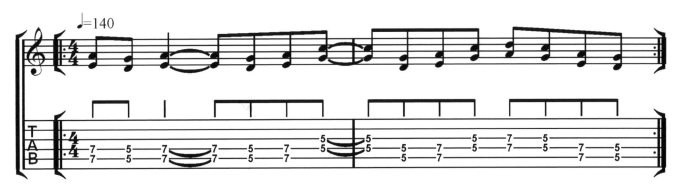

The next example teaches you how to play a low, shuffling Em riff. This idea could easily come from Black Sabbath or the later 'stoner' metal bands like Kyuss. It shows the enduring influence of early metal.

The musical distance from the root of a scale to the b5 (for example E to Bb) is called a *tritone*. When played in isolation, a tritone has a very dark and dissonant character and can create a sinister or 'evil' sound.

To hear an isolated tritone interval, listen to the intro to Jimi Hendrix's *Purple Haze*, or Black Sabbath's *Black Sabbath*.

We will look more closely at how to use the tritone effectively in riff writing later on.

**Example 1e:**

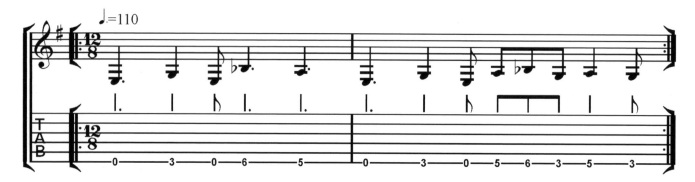

**Building Riffs with Pentatonic Scales**

The following ideas look at some other pentatonic scale shapes that can be used to create new riffs and ideas.

You might already be familiar with the pentatonic 'box' shapes that guitarists often use. These scales are very effective when developing lead guitar vocabulary, but they can also be used in a different way to create metal guitar riffs.

Metal guitar riffs are usually played on the lowest strings of the guitar, so for the moment we will focus there and learn to play up and down the length of these strings.

The following example shows the E Minor Pentatonic scale played on the low E string. If you learn to recognise the shape and sequence of these *intervals*, it will be beneficial for both your playing and fretboard knowledge.

**Example 1f:**

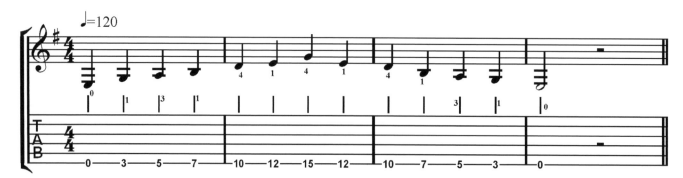

Example 1g shows how this single string approach can be used in a musical way. Notice how the subtle slides help to smooth the position shifts as well as making the riff more musical. The whole riff can be fingered with just the index and ring fingers.

**Example 1g:**

Staying on just the low E string helps us to keep the thick, consistent tone that is often important for metal rhythm guitar.

Many different ideas can be created by reordering the notes and using different phrasing.

Now that we know how E minor pentatonic sounds on the bottom string, we can extend the scale across the bottom three strings. Notice that each fragment contains the same five notes starting from a different point each time.

**Example 1h:**

Fluency in both horizontal and vertical patterns allows you to navigate all over the fretboard while staying within the E minor pentatonic scale.

Let's combine the previous two exercises and ascend from the open E string up to the fourteenth fret.

**Example 1i:**

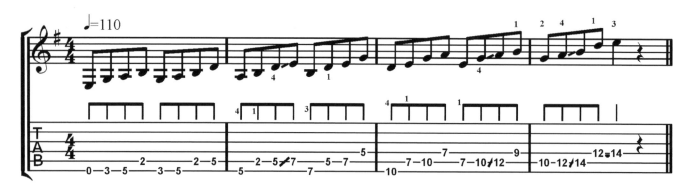

Try exploring these different pentatonic shapes by coming up with your own riffs as well as playing them as written. An interesting approach to building classic groovy riffs is to start strumming a rhythm with muted notes, and, as you repeat it over and over, gradually introduce pentatonic notes to the groove until you've got a loop that feels good and balances rhythmic and melodic interest.

## The Classic Roots of Modern Metal

You can hear a strong blues and hard rock influence in Tom Morello's approach to riff writing with Audio Slave. Dimebag Darrell also used pentatonic-based writing in Pantera. This bluesy 'swagger', combined with modern guitar tone and virtuosic delivery was why Pantera had such a huge impact on metal in the early '90s.

In the following riff the movement down the fretboard in bar one can be tricky, however, most of the notes can be played with the index and ring fingers while adding the pinkie for the Bb in bar one and the middle finger for the Bb in bar two.

**Example 1j:**

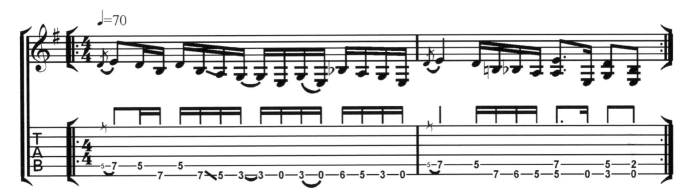

Example 1k lays down another linear riff in A minor that shifts the previous ideas up by one string and uses other ideas we've touched on, such as the b5, slides and double-stops. Be careful with the slides and pay attention to the recommended fingerings in bars three and four. This riff works in the key of D by moving it up by a string.

**Example 1k:**

**The following examples from early '70s hard rock to modern metal all use pentatonic based riffs:**

Led Zeppelin – *Heartbreaker*

Black Sabbath – *Iron Man*

Metallica – *Seek & Destroy*

Pantera – *I'm Broken*

Audioslave – *Cochise*

# Chapter Two: Moving Power Chords

*Power chords* consist of two notes: the root and the fifth. These two notes sound extremely stable together so a power chord sounds like a denser, reinforced version of the root note.

This *consonance* (musical stability) makes power chords work well with distortion and helps to avoid the 'mushiness' that can occur when full major or minor chords are played with distortion.

Power chords are normally one of the first things that modern guitarists learn, and there are thousands of rock songs that can be played using power chords alone. As well as being used to outline chord progressions, power chords are used to thicken up single-note riffs.

Playing riffs with power chords takes more coordination than simply holding a chord for a whole bar. This chapter will discuss some exercises and riffs that will help you to develop this skill.

Aim to maintain the shape of the power chord when sliding from one to the next by locking the fingers in position and moving the whole arm from the elbow. These first few exercises may seem simple, but they are an important rhythm guitar technique.

In the first example, we're simply sliding from a G power chord up to A. The important thing to notice is that the open E string is muted with the heel of the picking hand as it's played, but the chords are allowed to ring properly. This gives a sense of depth and contrast to the part.

**Example 2a:**

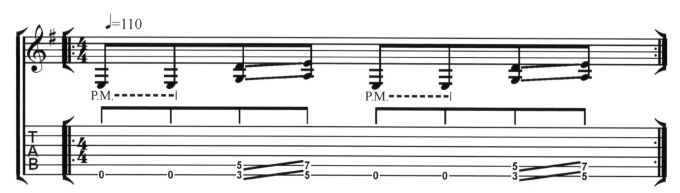

In the next example, the slide direction is reversed and the slide starts on an offbeat. Timing can be an issue with these slides because they are played *legato* (without picking) and many players rely on their picking hand to control the rhythm. Any rhythm guitar idea needs to be rhythmically tight so as to lock in with the bass and drums, so develop this accuracy early on.

**Example 2b:**

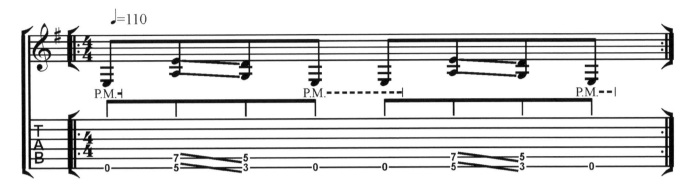

Next, we widen the intervals and include both ascending and descending slides. If you find you have difficulty stopping accurately at the right fret, it can be helpful to look at the target fret ahead of time, rather than just watching your hand play the first chord.

**Example 2c:**

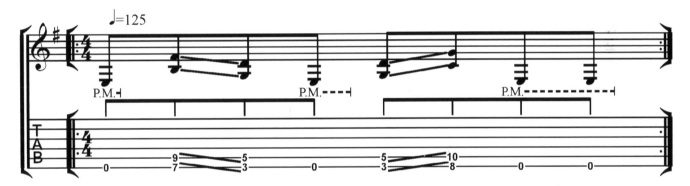

The following example groups slides together. Follow the picking directions to begin with, then for an extra challenge, pick only the first power chord in each group of four and slide each of the following ones. This approach can lose the forcefulness that metal guitar requires but it is a great way of testing your timekeeping.

**Example 2d:**

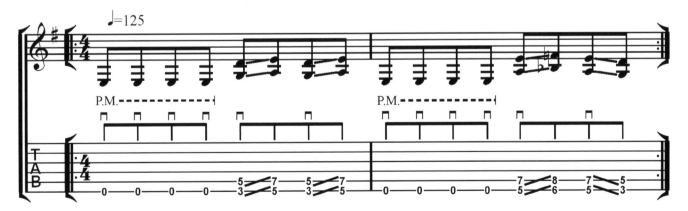

This next exercise uses sliding ideas along the length of the bottom strings. Take it slowly and remember to keep your eyes ahead of your hand if you're over- or under-shooting the slides.

**Example 2e:**

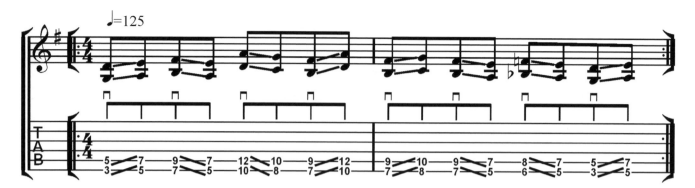

The final exercise demands some long slides up and down the neck and will help you to develop your accuracy. Dimebag Darrell had an excellent sliding technique, and could fly up and down the neck with precision while rocking out on stage. Test yourself by looking away from the guitar neck as you play and trust your ears to judge whether you've hit the right fret. This pays dividends when it's time to perform!

**Example 2f:**

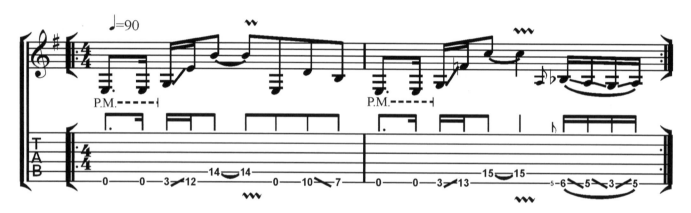

### Moving Chords Across Strings

Next we will work on moving power chord shape across strings. Despite the smaller distance, this movement can be harder than moving the chord along the length of one string because when changing chords, the fingers must briefly leave the strings, although keeping the shape of the power chord intact is essential.

**Example 2g:**

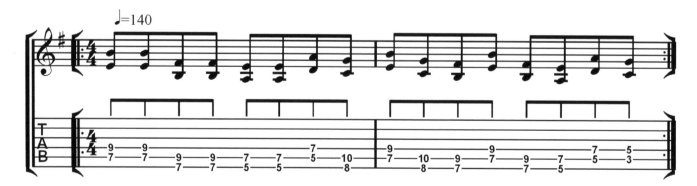

Example 2h is a slightly trickier example that builds upon exercise 2g by moving one fret *and* one string between each chord. Begin by carefully learning the chord movements at a slow tempo.

**Example 2h:**

You can hear ideas like this executed with speed and precision in death metal and other related genres. Aim to move the hand as little as possible. Keeping the fingers close to the strings helps with speed.

In the following example, we move along the neck in semitones while using an open E string *pedal*.

**Example 2i:**

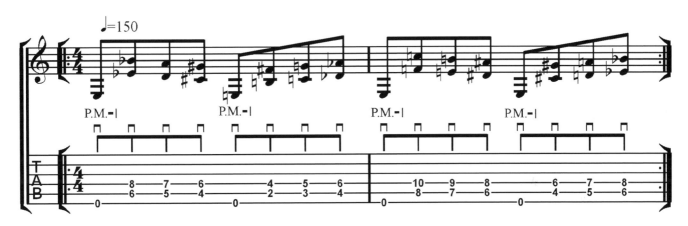

Try to *palm mute* the E string while allowing the chords to ring fully. Listen to the audio example to hear this technique in action. Down-picking the chords creates a more aggressive attack.

Finally, here's a chromatic death metal riff. Learn this idea slowly and focus on the timing. It is easy to become tense in the fretting hand, so if you feel yourself getting tight, be sure to shake it off and try again at a slower tempo. With consistent practice, stamina will build within a few weeks.

**Example 2j:**

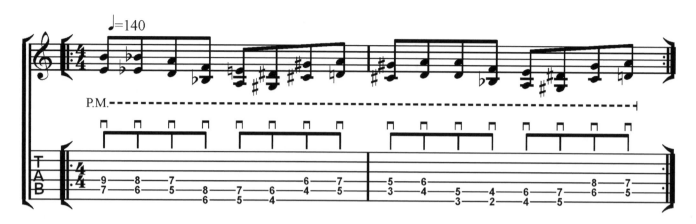

**The following songs feature moving power chord based riffs:**

Black Sabbath – *N.I.B.*

Metallica – *Master of Puppets* (verse)

Slayer – *Reborn*

Pantera – *A New Level*

Slipknot – *Surfacing* (bridge)

Machinehead – *Imperium* (chorus)


You can download all the audio in this book for free from **www.fundamental-changes.com/download-audio.**

# Chapter Three: Developing the Picking Hand

Over the past thirty years, metal's technical demands have required an increasingly well-developed picking hand.

This chapter gives you musical examples and exercises that develop the speed and stamina to tackle rhythm parts in thrash and death metal.

There are as many variations of picking hand position as there are players, but the most successful guitarists tend to have similar approaches.

The two essential considerations of any technique are a *relaxed posture* and *good sound*. By this, I mean that you should try to reduce any tension in your arms and hands while producing a quality of sound that has good clarity and attack.

When learning to play metal, there is a temptation to play fast straight away. Many young players cramp up and hunch over the guitar in an effort to replicate the speed they hear on records, but speed is the product of regular practice over a long period of time.

Repetitive strain injuries in the picking hand are not uncommon amongst extreme metal guitarists although this risk is greatly reduced by warming up properly and keeping the muscles relaxed while playing.

The powerful string attack of players like Jeff Hanneman (Slayer) and Chuck Schuldiner (Death) is the product of *relaxed* control. Sheer aggression is no substitute for relaxation and good technique.

The motion of the picking hand should come from the wrist rather than the thumb and index finger joints. Strumming from the wrist will allow more stamina than relying on the small muscles controlling each finger to move the pick.

Experiment with the angle of the pick as it makes contact with the strings. If the angle is too flat, the string will create too much resistance. If the pick strikes edge on, the note will be less clear. Many metal players prefer a thicker, 2mm pick with a sharp tip to put momentum behind the attack and glide through the strings.

When playing rhythm guitar you (along with the bass and drums), are a part of the band's rhythm section. For this reason timekeeping is your primary concern and is actually more important than tone or even note accuracy!

In rock and metal, it is standard practice for each rhythm guitar part to be *double-tracked* when recording. The doubled recordings result in a rich, fat sound that one guitar alone cannot achieve. However, if you try to record double tracking parts by yourself, the accuracy needed to record even a straightforward riff is raised significantly.

To help develop your sense of rhythm, always practice with a metronome or drum loop. This will get you used to playing to an external beat rather than at whatever speed happens to feel most comfortable to you.

There are two components to timekeeping:

- Keeping the tempo even.

- Subdividing the beat evenly.

As your picking technique gets more accurate and confident, the accuracy of your subdivisions will get better. However, keeping a consistent *internal* pulse is much less about physical technique and can be improved with simple exercises and a slow metronome.

## Internal Rhythm Exercises

Begin by strumming a simple acoustic-style rhythm to a metronome set at 160bpm. Tapping your foot can help with timekeeping by providing a regular pulse.

**Fig. 1:**

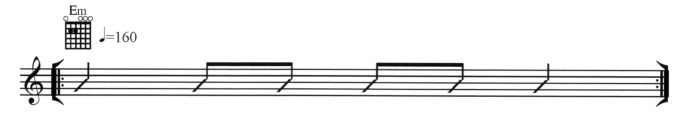

Once you feel that your playing at 160bpm is solid, set the metronome to 80bpm, but *play at the same speed.*

**Fig. 2:**

Half the click again to 40bpm. The click is now only heard on beat one of the bar and playing accurately with the slow click this slow can feel like a trust exercise. Staying in time can be hard at first but this kind of practice quickly improves your internal clock and helps you to be confident and relaxed.

**Fig. 3:**

Finally, set the metronome to 20bpm so that the click is only heard once every two bars. It will probably take you some time to get the feel of this exercise.

**Fig. 4:**

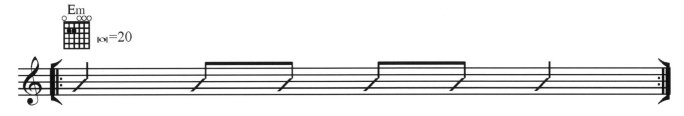

Some metronomes will not click this slowly but several smartphone apps and more expensive electronic metronomes have the option to click on only beat one of a bar.

If you can relax enough to play the previous exercises accurately without speeding up, you can feel confident in your time keeping.

Get into the habit of recording your practice and listening back to the results 24 hours later to make any timing issues more obvious. When you learn a new song, record it to objectively review your performance and to document your progress.

**Picking Riffs**

Now we've had a quick primer on timing and using a metronome, it's time to break out some metal riffs. These riffs have all been written to hone in on your picking hand and address the different issues that crop up in metal.

The following exercise uses constant 1/8th notes. Use all down-strokes rather than alternate picking to get an authentic, heavy metal attack.

**Example 3a:**

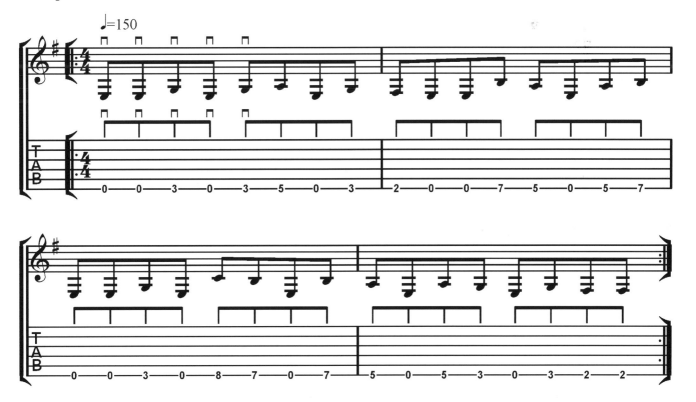

Palm muting helps to keep riffs tight and well articulated, and to create the characteristic 'chug' sound of metal rhythm guitar. To get the right sound, keep the fleshy side of your picking hand on the bridge saddles so that they touch and slightly mute the strings. Experiment by moving your hand further forward over the strings to increasingly dampen their ringing.

A good sound will allow you to hear the pitch of the notes but not have them ring out.

This second example introduces some notes on the A string. Maintaining the even down-strokes while changing strings takes a bit more control than just thrashing away at one string, so make sure you're relaxed and the wrist is free to slide across the bridge saddles.

**Example 3b:**

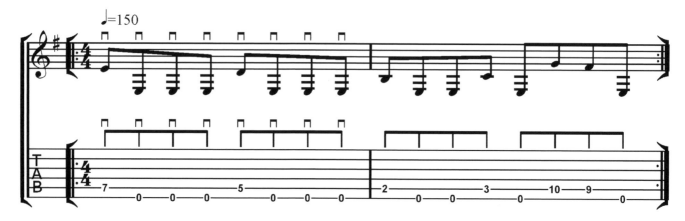

There are limitless possibilities for this kind of riff. Just have a listen to a handful of old school thrash metal records to hear different takes on the same idea.

The following down-picked riff involves more string crossing than the previous idea so practice this example slowly and learn to play it consistently before speeding up. Use all four fingers of the fretting hand to navigate the *chromatic* notes.

**Example 3c:**

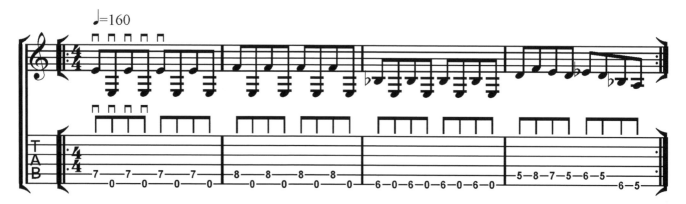

Gaining the speed and endurance needed for thrash metal takes time and repetition. Try raising the metronome speed periodically by 5bpm to see if you can maintain control at faster speeds. If you have any pain or lasting aches, you should see a doctor or a specialist. If you have any doubts, stop and get professional advice from your physician.

This next exercise is the foundation of everything that follows in this chapter so it's worth spending some time getting comfortable playing it at a moderate tempo of between 100 and 120bpm. Return to this exercise as you progress through the rest of the examples and you'll feel how your control improves.

The purpose of the exercise is to rhythmically 'lock in' and be aware of how each note subdivides the beat into four equal divisions. Start slowly, and accent the first of each four-note group to help stay in time as you begin to raise the metronome speed.

**Example 3d:**

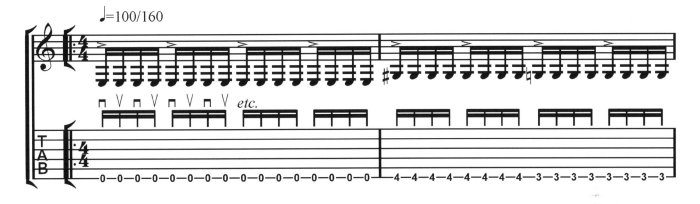

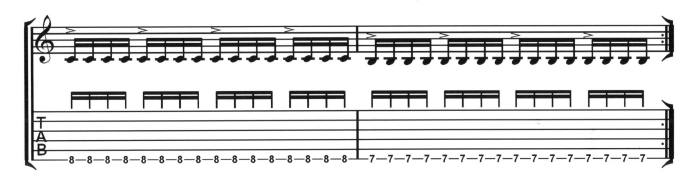

When playing the above example along with the audio, there should be unity between the bass drum hits and the guitar. The more you can concentrate on listening to the drums while you play, you more you'll be able to lock in.

## Gallop Rhythms

The 'gallop' rhythm has been played by many bands but is often associated with Iron Maiden who used it as the basis for several of their most famous songs.

Single string picking works just like strumming, so maintain the 1/16th note down/up pattern of exercise 3d to help your timing, and 'ghost' over the string when a note is not required. As the second pick of each four-note group is missed out, the picking pattern will be 'Down-Down-Up' on each beat.

**Example 3e:**

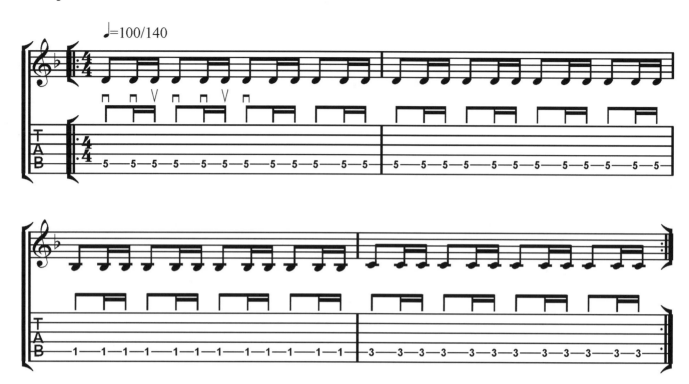

Let's use this idea to create some actual music. Using exercises to make music helps to keep us focused, enthusiastic and helps us to see a genuine creative benefit.

Adding power chords to the gallop rhythms highlights each chord change, driving the music forward.
**Example 3f:**

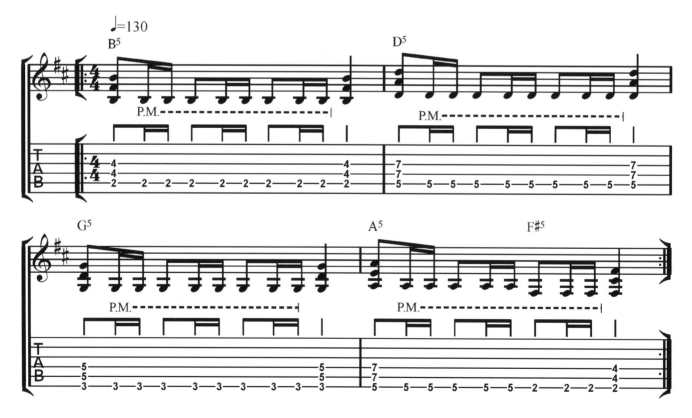

Keep the single notes tight and controlled while making the power chords big and loud. Achieve this by palm-muting the faster 'gallop' parts, but remove the palm from the bridge for the power chords and allow them to ring out fully.

Here's another riff that employs the gallop rhythm, but this time the open E string acts as a *pedal* (a static bass note) while the power chords provide melodic interest. Learn this riff slowly until both hands feel comfortable. Try to keep the power chord shape intact while sliding it around the neck and pay attention to the timing of the slides.

**Example 3g:**

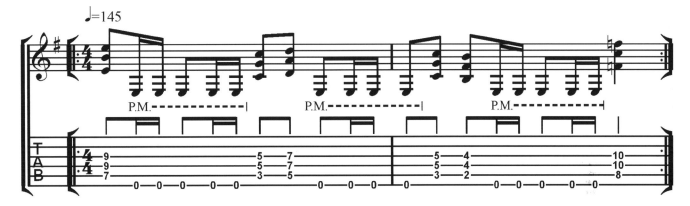

This kind of idea is common in '80s-era Metallica and Exodus, as well as with many other thrash metal bands.

Thrash metal fused together the sounds of British heavy metal and hardcore punk to create a fast-paced, aggressive new style incorporating the technical proficiency of metal. Thrash bands used a variation of the gallop rhythm known as the 'reverse gallop'.

By playing the reverse gallop pattern directly on the beat they created an energetic sense of urgency.

**Example 3h:**

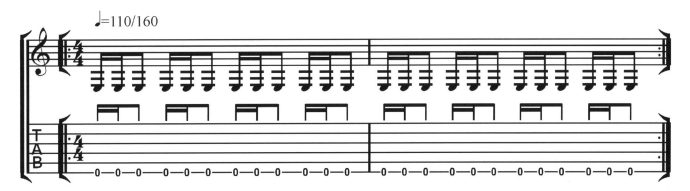

This idea may be a little more demanding, but your stamina should increase within a few weeks of playing these ideas regularly.

The next example is in 3/4 time, meaning that each bar contains three beats. More progressive bands from the early thrash movement, like Testament, as well as later bands like Death and Nevermore, use different time signatures to add variation to the thrash vocabulary. Keep the pick moving down and up in 1/16th notes.

**Example 3i:**

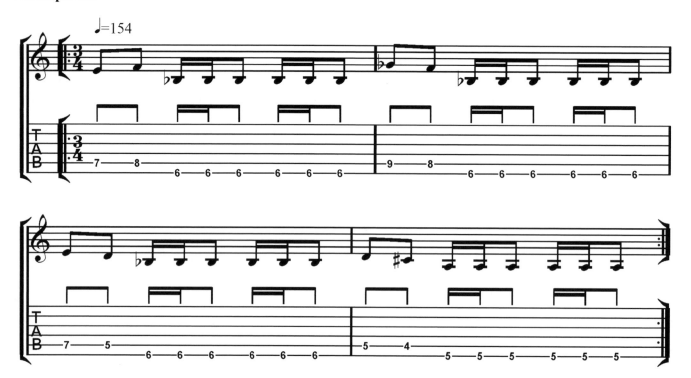

Example 3j again uses the reverse gallop pattern. Try to maintain down-strokes for the 1/8th notes on beats three and four. Down-strokes provide a more powerful tone, while the more consistent picking hand motion helps with timing.

**Example 3j:**

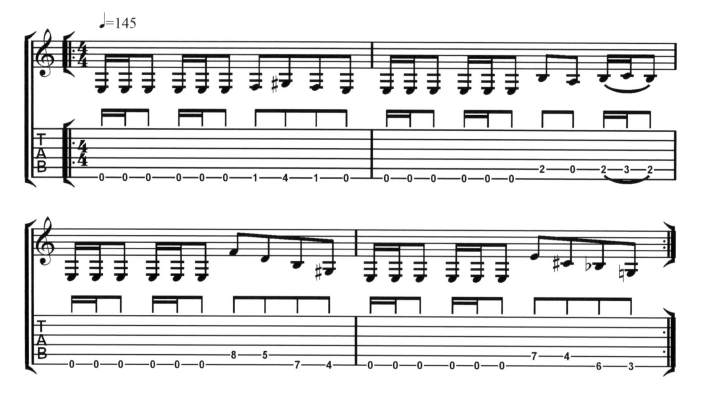

This combination of reverse gallop rhythm and dark note choices is often found in the music of Slayer.

Now for a more syncopated example in the style of Pantera.

Many of the notes in the following example occur on off-beats, so use strict alternate picking and follow the notated picking directions. To articulate the syncopated rhythms properly the notes should be kept short and punchy. Listen to the audio examples to help you capture the right feel.

**Example 3k:**

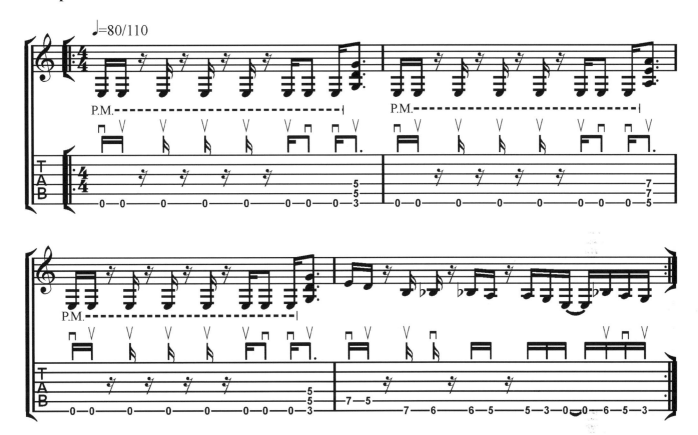

Between each note, mute the strings with the fretting hand by flattening the fingers gently across the strings. It may take some time to coordinate the hands, but go slowly and it will soon feel natural to switch between picking and muting.

Rhythmic precision was heightened by bands such as Fear Factory and Meshuggah in the early '90s and the next example demonstrates this style.

**Example 3l:**

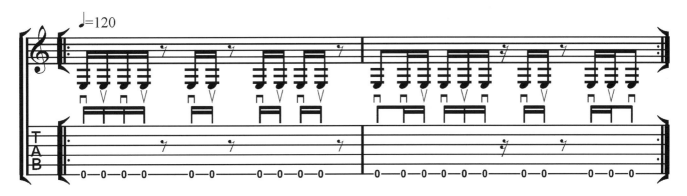

The gaps between the notes should be silent to create the proper impact.

For the most effective muting technique, rest the first finger of the picking hand on the top five strings throughout the riff and pad the remaining three fingers on to the strings to damp the sixth string during the rests. Fan the fingers to avoid accidental natural harmonics.

The technical bar for extreme metal rhythm playing was raised by Death and Cynic who both emerged from the late '80s Florida death metal scene. Cynic's debut album, *Focus* contains many technical and precise riffs.

The following two examples combine to form one musical idea that demonstrates the multi-layered approach to songwriting found across Cynic's records.

The first part shows a typical melodic idea where the motif is phrased in 1/8th notes, but each note is picked twice to create a 1/16th note pulse.

To help you hear the two parts more clearly these examples are played individually and then together.

**Example 3m:**

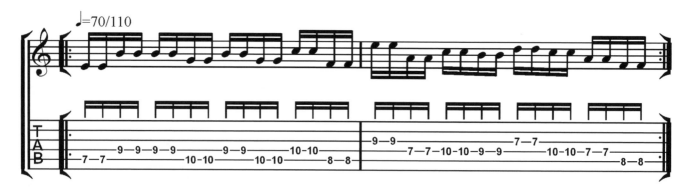

The lower guitar part, shown in example 3n, needs careful muting between the chords and single notes. The short bursts of 1/32nd notes must be given special attention too. The picking hand will need to be very relaxed to execute these rhythms comfortably and they should feel like a single, quick burst of energy.

**Example 3n:**

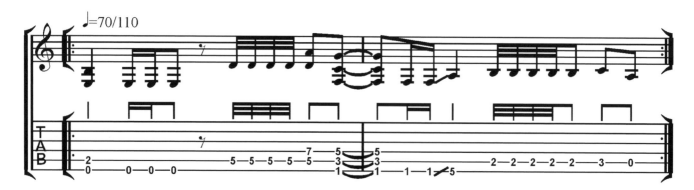

**The following songs contain great examples of these picking patterns in context:**

Iron Maiden – *The Trooper*

Anthrax – *Caught in a Mosh*

Metallica – *Motorbreath*

Megadeth – *Holy Wars... The Punishment Due*

Slayer – *Raining Blood*

Trivium – *Pull Harder on the Strings of Your Martyr*

# Chapter Four: Scales for Metal

Having looked at rhythmic patterns and phrasing in the previous chapters, we will now look at how scales add a melodic dimension to metal riffs.

Ever since Tony Iommi hit a tritone interval in the title track of Black Sabbath's eponymous debut album, heavy metal has been characterised by its dark, malicious-sounding music. This heavy sound created the perfect atmosphere for metal's brooding, aggressive or even satanic lyrics.

In this chapter, we will study the most commonly used scales in metal, and see how they are used by heavy metal rhythm guitarists to develop riffs and chord progressions.

Most scale dictionaries are usually designed for soloists and provide many patterns that cover the whole neck. As we are only concerned with rhythm guitar, the diagrams in this chapter teach scales on the lower (bass) strings and show how they're played horizontally along the neck. I have, however, included one 'open-position' scale shape across all six strings to help you build riffs in the lower portion of the neck.

When learning new scales, it is important to recognise each scale's defining 'character notes'. Every scale has a distinctive flavour, and knowing which notes contribute to the scale's unique mood is very important.

Most of the scales here contain the same minor chord (1, b3, 5) or minor pentatonic scale (1, b3, 4, 5, b7) within their seven notes, so the character notes are normally the remaining notes (the 2nd and the 6th).

It is useful to examine common chord progressions associated with each scale, both to help you make music, and also to see scales as a basis for songs rather than just theoretical ideas. To form chords from scales, each scale needs to be *harmonised*.

**Harmonising a Scale**

Chords are formed by stacking up three notes, each a 3rd above the previous one. These three-note structures are called *triads* and they are the most basic type of chord structure in music.

To harmonise a (C Major) scale start with the notes of C major written out:

C D E F G A B C

To build a chord on each step simply take alternate notes.

**C** D **E** F **G** A B C  = C,E,G = major triad

As you can see, a triad is formed by skipping alternate notes in the scale, and this process can be started on any note in the scale.

The notes C, E and G form the chord of C major while the notes D, F and A form the chord of D minor. The distance from C to E is four semitones, but the distance from D to F is only three semitones.

C **D** E **F** G **A** B C

If a triad has a distance of *four semitones* between the root and the 3rd (e.g., C to E), then it is a major chord. If a triad has a distance of *three semitones* between the root and the 3rd (e.g., D to F), it is a minor chord.

Forming triads on each note in the scale creates the following sequence of chords:

C major, D minor, E minor, F major, G major, A minor, B diminished

Chords are often referred to by Roman numerals. Each chord is referred to by its relationship to the root of the parent scale.

In Roman numerals the Major scale is written in the following way:

I      ii      iii      IV      V      vi      vii°

Capital letters indicate major chords and lower case letters indicate minor chords.

In the above diagram, you can see that chord I is major, (capital letters) but chord vi is minor (lower case).

Every Major scale has the same pattern of intervals therefore the sequence of major and minor triads will be the same in every key. This means the Roman numerals can represent the notes found on the steps of any scale.

*Diminished* triads (chords built from two minor thirds) are indicated by a small circle and *augmented* triads (chords built from two major thirds) are shown by a plus (+) sign.

Other scales are formed with a different pattern of intervals, so later you will see chords being referred to by sharps and flats (#'s and b's). For example, you may see chord bIII. This symbol tells us that the third step of the scale is a minor third from the root and that the chord formed on it is major.

Using this system, I'll illustrate the chords formed when each of the scales in this chapter is harmonised and also suggest some chord progressions for you to experiment with.

# The Natural Minor / Aeolian Mode

Aeolian or 'Natural' minor has a sombre yet majestic quality and is the most common seven-note minor scale used in metal. Guitarists such as Gary Moore, Richie Blackmore and Uli Jon Roth started using this scale in the '70s to expand the bluesy vocabulary of hard rock at that time.

The natural minor scale provides many strong chord progressions and is usually the basis for minor-key songs. The sombre quality of the scale occurs because the harmonised scale creates a minor v chord, rather than the major V chord provided by the closely related Harmonic Minor scale.

The character notes are the natural 2nd and b6th of the scale. Moving from the 2nd up to the b3rd, or from the b6th to the 5th step of the scale with a melody or riff will help you to hear Aeolian's dark mood clearly. Our musical examples home in on these specific intervals.

### E Aeolian/Natural Minor: Formula 1 2 b3 4 5 b6 b7

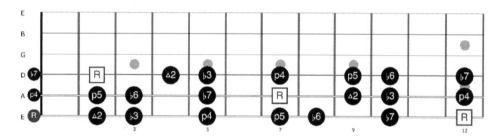

### E Aeolian/Natural Minor

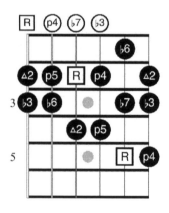

### The Aeolian mode harmonised:

| i | ii° | bIII | iv | v | bVI | bVII |
|------|-------|------|------|------|------|------|
| Em | F#dim | G | Am | Bm | C | D |

**Common Chord Progressions:**

**Songs that use the Aeolian mode:**

Metallica – *Fade to Black*

Iron Maiden – *The Loneliness of the Long Distance Runner*

Judas Priest – *Breaking the Law*

Ozzy Osbourne – *Crazy Train*

Muse – *Time is Running Out*

Rammstein – *Reise, Reise*

Slipknot – *Sulfur*

The first example is written in the style of British heavy metal bands like Iron Maiden and Judas Priest. It outlines a common rock guitar progression and ends with a scale fill that highlights the character notes of the Aeolian mode.

**Example 4a:**

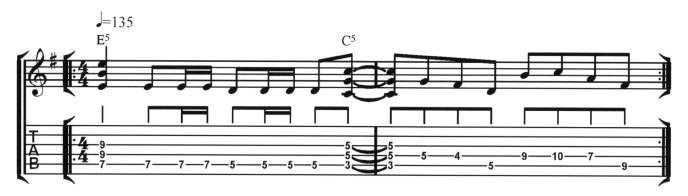

The following riff is a repeating, one-bar pattern that outlines the Aeolian mode while a second guitar uses power chords to play an Aeolian chord progression.

When playing with another guitarist, take the time to arrange complementary parts rather just playing in unison.

**Example 4b:**

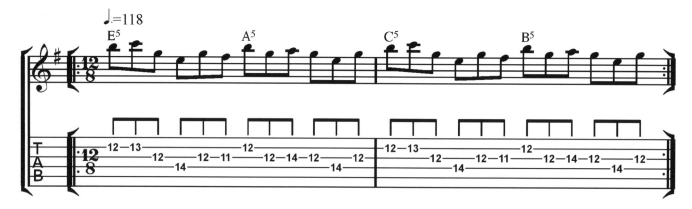

Listen to the way Hetfield and Hammett use the two guitars to complement each other in classic Metallica songs, creating a more interesting texture.

The third Aeolian riff is in the style of more melodic bands like The Offspring or Rufio, who mixed melodic post-hardcore punk and metal in the '90s. Use downstrokes for a driving rhythmic sound. Some palm muting on the bass notes will help to emphasise the melody.

**Example 4c:**

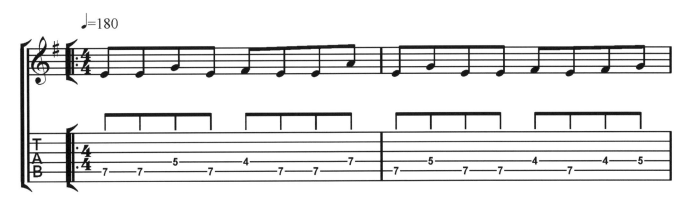

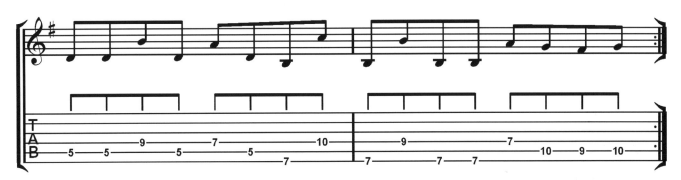

Notice also how the lowest note changes throughout the riff while the overall rhythmic pattern stays the same. This implies a sense of moving harmony through the riff, which could be further developed by effective bass guitar writing.

# The Harmonic Minor Scale

The Harmonic Minor scale is very popular in the neoclassical style that was pioneered by Uli Jon Roth, Richie Blackmore and Yngwie Malmsteen in the '80s. These players combined metal guitar with a vocabulary drawn from classical composers such as Nicolo Paganini and J.S. Bach. The neoclassical style influenced heavy metal, and the Harmonic Minor scale is now used by many players.

The Harmonic Minor scale provides a sense of classical influence, as well as a hint of exoticism created by the tone-and-a-half interval between its b6 and 7th degree. Harmonic Minor differs from the natural minor scale by only one note (the 7th note is raised), but this causes a dramatic change in its flavour and the chords generated when it is harmonised.

The raised 7th turns the previously minor v chord into a (dominant) V7 chord, and the V7 – i chord progression is a big factor in the neoclassical sound of the Harmonic Minor scale. A diminished chord exists on the second degree of the scale (ii°), so diminished arpeggios are often heard in Harmonic Minor tunes. The character notes of Harmonic Minor are the b6 and the 7.

Be careful when playing the wider stretches found in this scale. Spreading your first and fourth fingers across five frets may seem uncomfortable at first, but your fingers will limber up with practice. Just be careful not to overstretch and damage your tendons.

### E Harmonic Minor Formula: 1 2 b3 4 5 b6 7

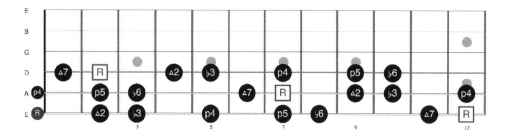

### E Harmonic Minor

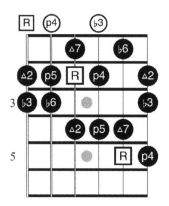

### The Harmonic Minor scale harmonised:

| i | ii° | bIII | iv | V7 | bVI | vii° |
|------|--------|------|------|------|------|--------|
| Em | F#dim | G | Am | B7 | C | D#dim |

**Common Chord Progressions:**

**Songs that use the Harmonic Minor scale:**

Yngwie Malmsteen – *Vengeance*

Muse – *New Born*

Pantera – *Revolution in My Name* (bridge)

Children of Bodom – *Bed of Razors*

Trivium – *Entrance of the Conflagration* (pre-chorus)

Sonata Arctica – *8th Commandment*

Our first riff moves from an E5 power chord to a D#5 to capture the flavour of the E Harmonic Minor scale. The short sequence of thirds in bar four helps to accentuate the neoclassical sound. Listen to the audio example and check out how I vary the palm muting throughout the riff.

Being able to control and vary your palm muting is an important skill and which helps to bring your music to life. The power chords should be unmuted, the repeated Es should be heavily muted, and the final phrase should be lightly muted so that the pitches are still clearly audible.

**Example 4d:**

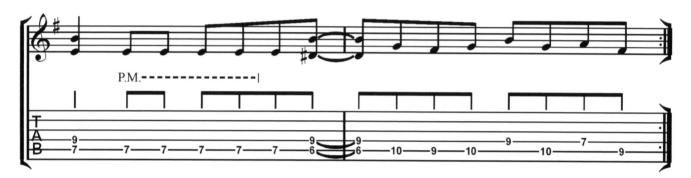

This next neoclassical-style riff is a great picking workout. Although the triplet feel gives the riff something of a swagger, the picking still needs to be precise and controlled. Note the inclusion of the diminished arpeggio in the last two beats of bar two. The Harmonic Minor scale can be implied by combining the tonic arpeggio (in this case E minor) with a diminished arpeggio played either a tone up or a semitone below the tonic (F#dim or D#dim).

**Example 4e:**

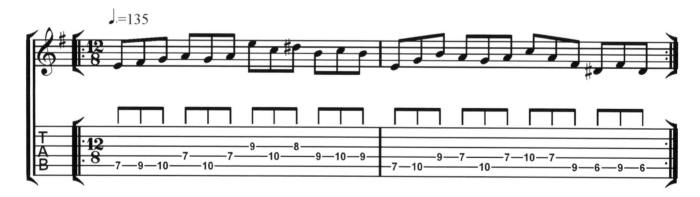

In the next riff, you may find the legato notes a little difficult to control at first, but these phrases help to break up the tonal consistency of the picking.

The semitone ideas target the b6 and natural 7th character notes of Harmonic Minor. In the second bar, the tension comes to a head as the accented notes form a descending B7 arpeggio (B A F# D#) that implies a progression of Em – B7 (i-V7)), typical of the Harmonic Minor harmony.

**Example 4f:**

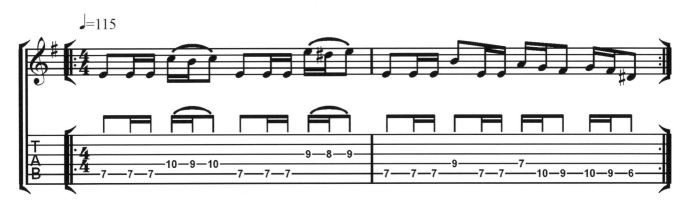

While the Harmonic Minor scale can be very effective in bringing a sense of drama to your playing, its distinctive flavour can become over-familiar if you're not careful. Be responsible and use in moderation!

# The Phrygian Mode

The Phrygian mode is similar to Aeolian except that the 2nd note of Phrygian is flattened. This small difference creates a unique character. The Phrygian mode is often found in Persian and Indian music and provides an exotic Eastern sound when used in metal.

**E Phrygian Formula: 1 b2 b3 4 5 b6 b7**

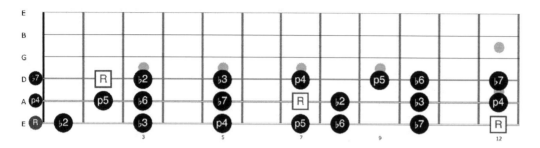

**E Phrygian**

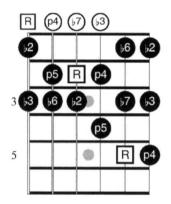

**The Phrygian mode harmonised:**

| i | bII | bIII | iv | v° | bVI | bvii |
|------|------|------|------|------|------|------|
| Em | F | G | Am | Bdim | C | Dm |

**Common Chord Progressions:**

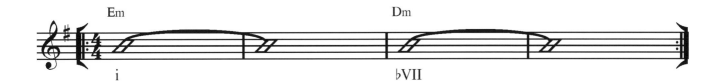

**Songs that use the Phrygian mode:**

Slipknot – *Duality*

Mastodon – *Blood and Thunder*

Megadeth – *Take no Prisoners*

Al di Meola – *Race with the Devil on a Spanish Highway*

Metallica – *Wherever I may Roam*

Here is a thunderous, heavy riff that exploits Phrygian's brooding b2 interval. The heaviest riffs are often the slow, dragging ones, rather than the ones that are fast and 'shredding'.

Dig in hard with your pick, and heavily palm mute the two 1/16th notes in bar one. Use wide vibrato on the final F and play it with attitude!

**Example 4g:**

Now for a typically aggressive riff akin to bands like Slayer and Exodus. Let the power chords ring clearly but palm mute the open low E string. The last beat could be picked but the legato provides a tonal contrast.

**Example 4h:**

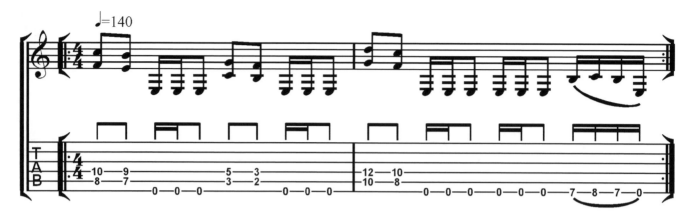

In the next example, try to keep the fretting hand locked into the octave shape when sliding around the fretboard just as we did with power chords in chapter two. The picking should be a loose strumming motion, so keep the other strings quiet by flattening the fretting hand index finger over the unused strings and releasing the pressure for the muted notes.

**Example 4i:**

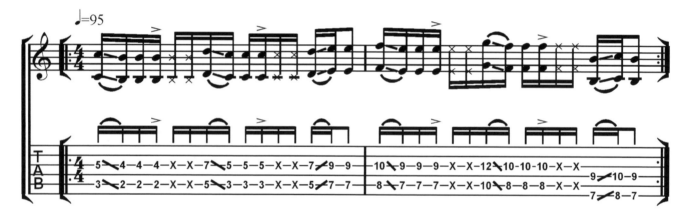

# The Phrygian Dominant Mode

The Phrygian Dominant mode was popular with the original crop of neoclassical rock guitarists, but can also be found in thrash and death metal due to the far-reaching influence of players like Yngwie Malmsteen, Marty Friedman and Jason Becker.

Phrygian Dominant is closely related to the Phrygian mode, the only difference being the presence of a major 3rd compared the minor Phrygian mode.

The name Phrygian *Dominant* arises because the scale is built on the *dominant* (5th) degree of the Harmonic Minor scale. Phrygian Dominant contains the same notes as the Harmonic Minor scale but beginning on the 5th. For example, E Phrygian Dominant contains the same notes as A Harmonic Minor, but E is heard as the 'home' note, rather than A.

It can be difficult to hear the difference between modes just from playing scale shapes. The flavour really becomes apparent when you play them over the appropriate chords.

The sound of this scale is more tense and restless than the Harmonic Minor scale.

## E Phrygian Dominant Formula: 1 b2 3 4 5 b6 b7

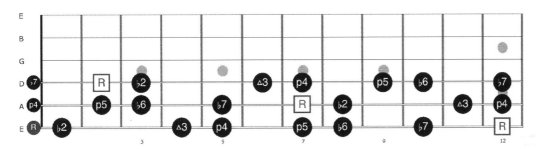

## E Phrygian Dominant

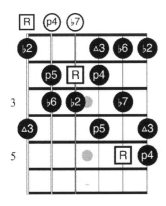

## The Phrygian Dominant mode harmonised:

| I7 | bII | biii° | iv | v° | bVI⁺ | bvii |
|----|-----|-------|-----|------|------|------|
| E7 | F | G#dim | Am | Bdim | Caug | Dm |

**Common Chord Progressions:**

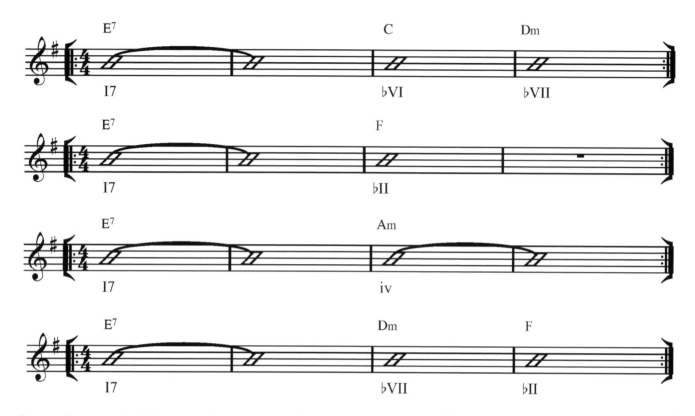

**Songs that use the Phrygian Dominant mode:**

The Scorpions – *Sails of Charon*

Symphony X – *Inferno (Unleash the Fire)*

Metallica – *Wherever I may Roam*

Death – *Pull the Plug*

The heavily distorted guitar tones used in metal can make full chords sound muddy and undefined when they are strummed, so using *arpeggios* to break up chords is a great approach. The following riff moves between some of the triads contained in the Phrygian Dominant scale. **Example 4j:**

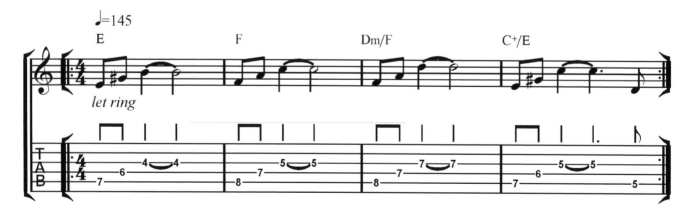

With slower arpeggios, note separation is less important than in melodic riffs, and allowing the notes to bleed into one another can be a useful creative effect. Roll down the volume on the guitar to make your amp/pedal provide less distortion for a bit more clarity.

The next riff is similar to Uli Jon Roth's work with The Scorpions. The 3, b2 and b6 of the scale are emphasised.

**Example 4k:**

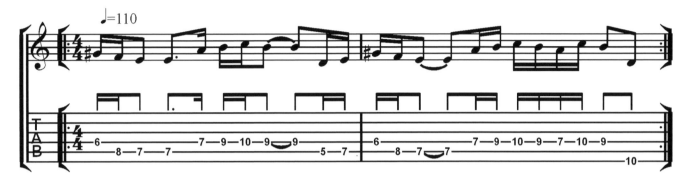

Our last Phrygian Dominant example highlights the adjacent major thirds (E-G# and F-A) contained within the scale. It then targets other major thirds in the scale before ending with a typical melodic turnaround.

**Example 4l:**

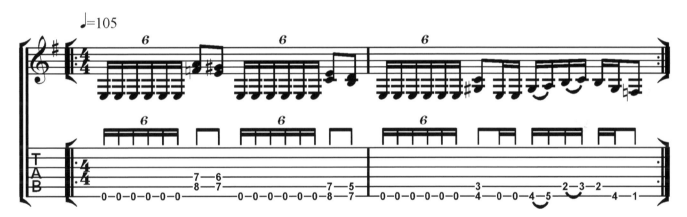

Keep the wrist loose for the fast picking 'cells'. You'll find that the sextuplets will take care of themselves if you focus on landing the final downstroke on the following beat. Angle the pick forward slightly to help slice through the string more easily.

# The Locrian Mode

The Locrian mode is often neglected in the study of music. It is not used in popular music due to its dark and dissonant harmony, although this dissonance and instability can be exploited to create menacing, demonic-sounding riffs!

The Locrian mode does not contain a natural 5th interval from the root, instead having a diminished 5th or *tritone* (during the middle ages the tritone was superstitiously known as the devil's interval) and because of this inherent instability, the Locrian mode is normally used in combination with other minor scales such as Phrygian or Aeolian. Mixing these related modes provides a whole spectrum of tensions.

The Aeolian, Phrygian and Locrian modes represent a wide range of stability and dissonance although just one note changes between each scale.

### E Locrian Formula: 1 b2 b3 4 b5 b6 b7

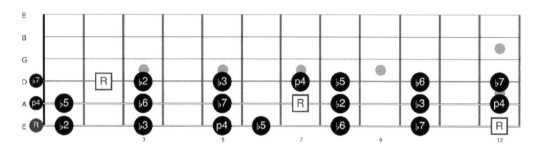

### E Locrian

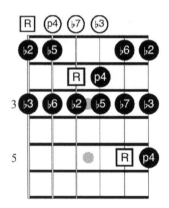

### The Locrian mode harmonised:

| i° | bII | biii | iv | bV | bVI | bvii |
|------|-----|------|-----|-----|-----|------|
| Edim | F | Gm | Am | Bb | C | Dm |

Having said earlier that character notes are not normally found in a scale's tonic chord, it's worth noting that in this case it's the presence of the b5 that differentiates Locrian from Phrygian, and creates Locrian's unresolved flavour.

**Common Chord Progressions:**

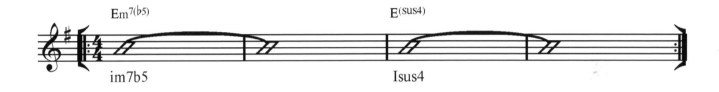

**Songs that use the Locrian mode:**

Metallica – *Seek and Destroy*

Slayer – *Angel of Death*

Metallica – *Blackened*

In example 4m the *tritone* (a distance of three tones) between the root and b5 is emphasised to bring out the full dissonance of the Locrian mode. The final bar uses two four-note patterns. First starting on the b5 and then on the b2.

Whether you decide to use down-picking or alternate picking, be sure to get the string crossing accurate.

**Example 4m:**

Norwegian Black Metal bands in the early '90s had a 'punk rock', lo-fi aesthetic to both their production and their playing. While these bands would have tremolo-picked the following riffs with less control, the bands that they influenced, such as Strapping Young Lad and Cryptopsy were much more technically precise. Aim for exact semiquavers here to lock in with the drum part.

**Example 4n:**

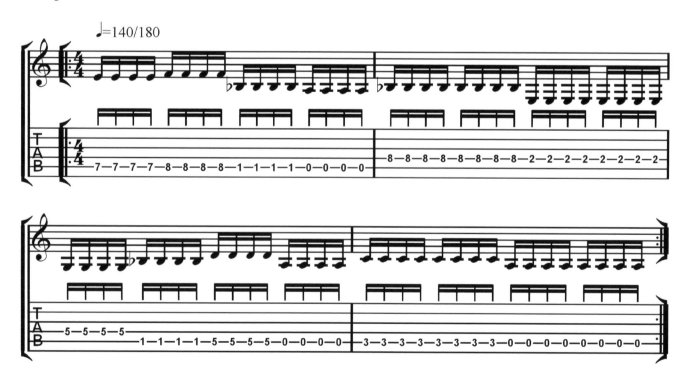

After that warp speed use of the Locrian mode, the following straight-ahead nu-metal inspired riff slows things down and focuses on groove and simplicity while leaning heavily on the tritone interval. The key to making this riff work is to really dig in with the pick to create a percussive sound. Lock in rhythmically with the drums to make it groove. It's almost like a heavy version of a funk guitar riff.

**Example 4o:**

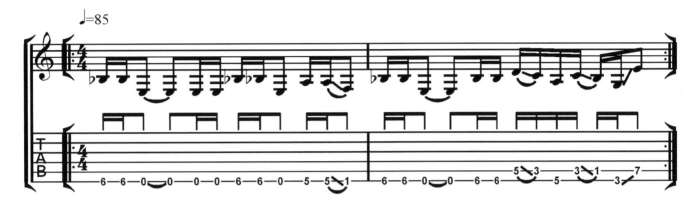

The nu-metal bands had the heaviness of metal but drew from alternative rock and grunge's sense of songwriting so they often avoided overly technical riffs, or lengthy instrumental sections. Many heavy metal fans and guitarists write off this whole subgenre but the change of aesthetic allowed a different range of influences to seep into metal.

# Diminished Seventh Arpeggios

The word 'arpeggio' is just a posh was of saying 'play the notes of a chord separately'. Arpeggios are treated as melodic devices just like scales and modes, except they have wider intervals between each note.

A *diminished seventh* chord (different from the diminished triad found in the Locrian mode) is a four-note chord with the intervals 1, b3, b5, bb7. All of the notes in the chord are a minor third apart.

When the notes in a chord are all the same distance apart it is referred to as a *symmetrical* chord. The musical benefit of this characteristic is that any diminished motif can be shifted up or down in minor thirds while still staying within the tonality.

Diminished arpeggios are not found in the major scale but occur in both the Harmonic Minor and Phrygian Dominant scales. Given their symmetrical nature, there are only three possible different diminished arpeggios before you repeat one in a different inversion.

## E Diminished Arpeggio: Formula 1 b3 b5 bb7

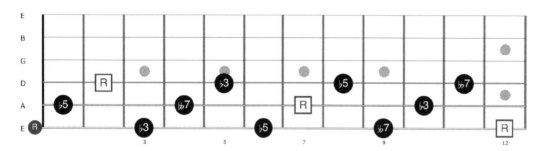

## E Diminished Arpeggio

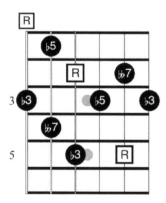

**Songs that use diminished arpeggios:**

Symphony X – *Seven*

Yngwie Malmsteen – *Arpeggios from Hell*

Nevermore - *Born*

Arch Enemy – *Nemesis* (bridge)

The following example shows that music theory is quite flexible when dissonance is the objective, and the strongly recognisable sound of the diminished arpeggio allows you to combine them at will without worrying about a parent scale or tonality. There are only three different diminished arpeggios (because each *inversion* is still a diminished arpeggio.) Rather than using all three, try picking two out of the three to maintain a cohesive but dissonant sound.

Example 4p combines the diminished arpeggios of E,G,Bb,C# and F#,A,C,D#, spending two beats on each before shifting from one to the other.

Using legato should help with the string crossing here but keep an eye on your timing!

**Example 4p:**

Jeff Loomis frequently used diminished ideas during his time with Nevermore, and this next riff is inspired by their earlier albums. In the next example, I wasn't thinking about a specific scale, even though the open E string gives a sense of tonal centre. The ear accepts the overall effect because of the distinct, recognisable pattern of each diminished arpeggio.

**Example 4q:**

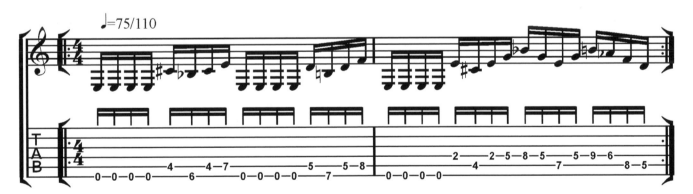

In example 4r, we use just one diminished arpeggio but move the same pattern up and down through its different inversions.

Although the pattern stays the same, notice how it is re-fingered in bar three to make the position shift at the start of bar four easier. The added open Es in bars three and four help with the position change, as well as providing variation to the riff pattern.

**Example 4r:**

To learn to use the diminished arpeggio with other scales, try combining riff ideas from Harmonic Minor or Phrygian Dominant with diminished arpeggios. From the harmonising and chord progression sections of each scale subchapter we can see that a diminished arpeggio is actually hidden within both those scales, so you should find that they flow one into the other nicely.

Good combinations to experiment with would be A Harmonic Minor with D diminished, or B Phrygian Dominant with C diminished.

# Mixing Scales

In practice, musicians often mix together several scales to create riffs from a chromatic palette of notes, and in thrash and death metal it is common to take a motif or a single interval and move it up or down in semitones.

Given that making interesting and exciting music is our goal, combining elements of different shapes and scales without worrying about 'correct theory' is as much of a legitimate approach as playing within the confines of one scale.

In the end, the only judge of good or bad is your ear and, to use an old cliché, 'if it sounds right, it is!'. Whether your compositions are built on theoretical understanding or not isn't really that important.

**Songs that mix scales or shift motifs up and down:**

Slayer – *Raining Blood*

Metallica – *Disposable Heroes*

Meshuggah – *Straws Pulled at Random*

Slipknot – *Surfacing*

Cynic – *Veil of Maya*

Megadeth – *Rust in Peace... Polaris*

Building on the previous diminished arpeggio examples (that strayed from the confines of a single key), the following examples are only concerned with the *effect* of each note over the E pedal.

It is possible to view our first example in terms of where the parts are borrowed from: Locrian (Bb, F), the Blues scale (B-Bb) and Aeolian (F#-G), but it makes more sense to just see semitone pairs moving around the root and to let your ear decide what works best.

**Example 4s:**

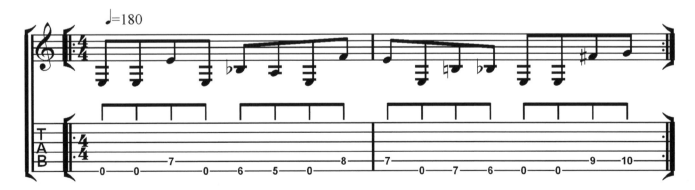

The next example is a James Hetfield inspired riff featuring power chords and down-picking. The riff includes chromatic movement but still outlines an E minor pattern.

Practice moving the power chords around accurately at a slower tempo because they can easily get out of control during long, fast phrases.

**Example 4t:**

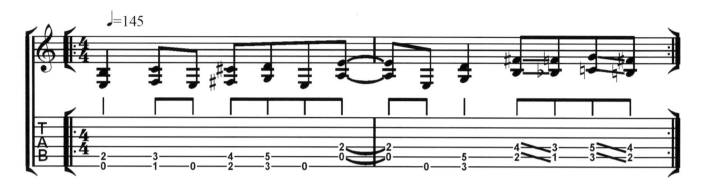

Our final example is in the style of bands like Slayer and Exodus. The motif in bars one and three is moved chromatically in the answering phrases in bars two and four. Getting the fingering tidy here can be a little tricky, so take it slowly to ensure you're using the most comfortable approach for you.

**Example 4u:**

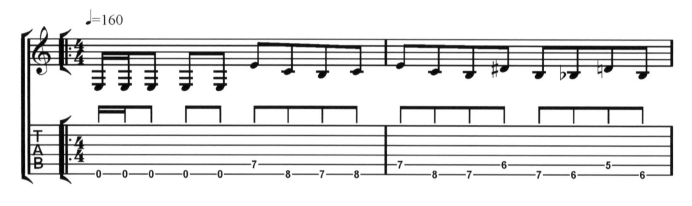

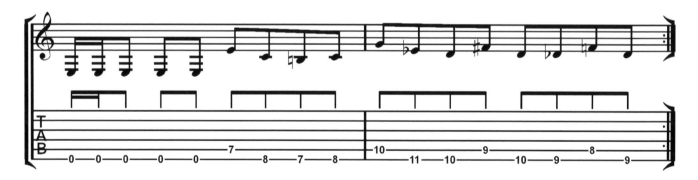

Hopefully this inspection of the various scales and arpeggios found in metal has given you a better understanding of how riffs are constructed, and why certain riffs sound the way they do. It's worth trying to think creatively and emotionally about this information, rather than getting swept up by all the theory. What does each scale's flavour make you think of, and does it makes you feel?

Keep your ears open for scales and modes as you work through the other chapters and identify the melodic devices used.

# Chapter Five: Harmonics

After all those chugging rhythms and sludgy power chords it's time for some contrast. When listening to metal, you've probably heard some high-pitched, piercing notes interspersed between the low riffs. These notes are called *harmonics*, and in this chapter we'll discuss different types of harmonics and how they're achieved.

Rhythm guitar playing can sometimes sound a bit sludgy and nebulous, particularly when the guitars are down-tuned to a lower register. Harmonics can break up this wall of sound and help to accentuate important beats.

## A brief physics lesson...

A guitar string vibrates to produce the sound we hear, and the rate at which it vibrates dictates the pitch of the note. However, to create the *tone* that you hear, strings also vibrate in a complex combination of higher frequencies simultaneously. These frequencies are known as harmonics or overtones.

The relative loudness of each overtone defines the perceived *timbre* of an instrument and allows our ears to distinguish the characteristics of notes played on different instruments (or between different strings on the guitar). This is why a clarinet sounds different from a cello when playing the same pitch.

The wavelength of the fundamental note is equal to the length of the string. The harmonic overtones vibrate in divisions of this length.

Without getting too scientific, a harmonic can only be found at *node* points along the string where the scale length can be divided into equal divisions or ratios. The following diagram illustrates why the harmonics fall where they do on the fretboard.

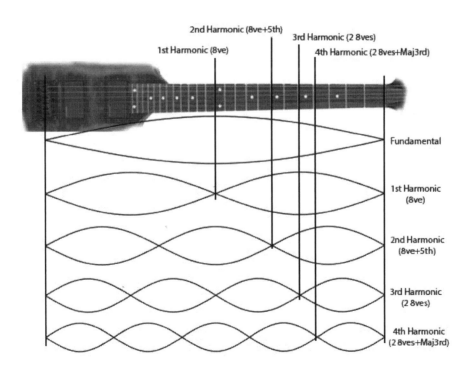

Harmonics are played by isolating the higher frequency overtones and removing the fundamental pitch of the open string by manipulating the strings at node points.

On the guitar, it is possible to create a range of natural and 'artificial' harmonics and these will be discussed in turn.

# Natural Harmonics

*Natural* harmonics are the most widely used harmonic and also the easiest to play. Natural harmonics are not found on every fret, they are only available at the *node* points as shown in the diagram. The strongest ones are at the 12th, 7th and 5th frets.

To perform a natural harmonic, gently touch the string at the 12th fret, but don't press down onto the fretboard. Make contact directly over the fret wire rather than behind it. When you pick the string the sound should be pure and bell-like.

Here is a preliminary figure to help you isolate the technique before working through the riffs. In the first bar lay the index finger across the whole fretboard, making sure that all the strings are ringing out and are not muted accidentally. In the second bar try to keep each harmonic separate by just using a smaller area of the pad of the finger. Remember, you are not fully fretting the note, just gently touching the string above the fret.

**Fig. 1**

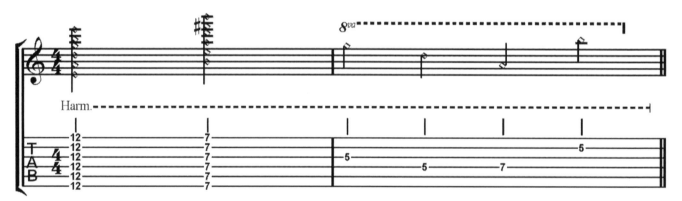

Our first riff is inspired by Slayer's South of Heaven/Seasons in the Abyss period and contrasts a chugging, muted riff with chiming bell-like natural harmonics.

Ringing harmonics can be beautiful when played with a clean tone, but they can easily get out of control when distortion is added. When combining riffs with harmonics, it's very important to mute the unplayed strings and learn to deaden harmonics after they have been played.

Use the palm of the picking hand and the unused fingers of the fretting hand to mute them.

**Example 5a:**

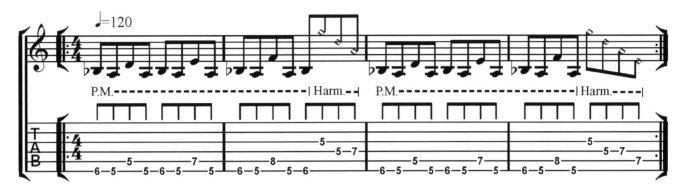

Use the pad of the first finger to play the fifth fret harmonics, aiming to place it across the strings so that it mutes the B while you play the G. It should also move to mute the G when playing the D string. Repeat the process with the ring finger on the seventh fret.

In the following example, we alternate a low, single-note riff with two different harmonics to build your control.

**Example 5b:**

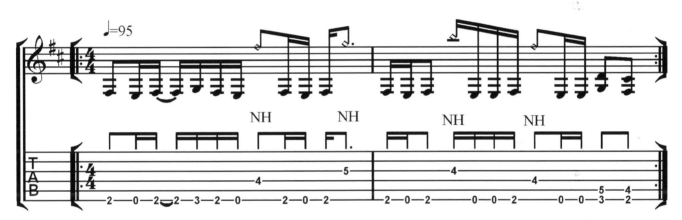

Use the pinkie to catch the harmonics while the first finger is laid across the bass strings to keep them silent. Take the time to find the position that works for your hand and neck profile.

The menacing feel of the following riff is enhanced by the inclusion of the haunting harmonics. The low E string can drone throughout and the harmonics will benefit by being allowed to overlap to create a suitably dark dissonance!

**Example 5c:**

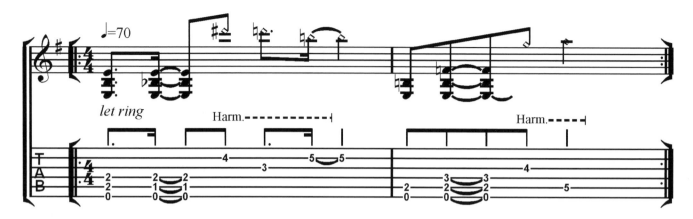

Harmonics at the fourth fret and below can be more difficult to execute than those at the 12th, 7th and 5th frets, but using distortion, the bridge pickup and picking near the bridge will all help the harmonics ring out successfully. These higher harmonics are demonstrated in example 5c.

The third-fret harmonic in bar one is played just in front of the fret wire, rather than directly over it because that is where the harmonic node falls. This slight mismatch between fret position and the harmonic node is a good illustration of how true intonation and our equal tempered system diverge.

The next harmonic idea is more of a sound effect than a proper riff so this technique is often used as an embellishment or fill.

We are going to play a series of natural harmonics by lightly brushing the E string between the neck pickup and highest frets.

Dimebag Darrell and Mark Tremonti (Alterbridge) have used this effect, and bassist Billy Sheehan often uses this idea in his unaccompanied bass solos with Mr Big and other bands.

**Example 5d:**

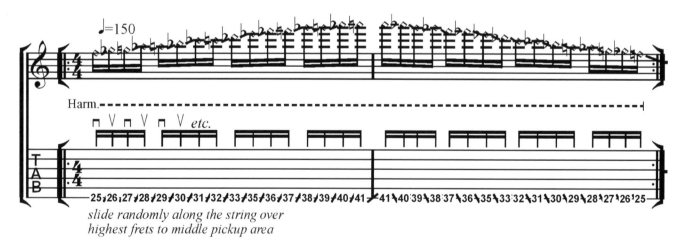

*slide randomly along the string over
highest frets to middle pickup area*

# Pinch Harmonics

Pinch harmonics (also affectionately known as 'squealies') are the most aggressive sounding harmonics. Unlike natural harmonics, they are created entirely by the picking hand, leaving the fretting free to add vibrato and bends to the pinched note. When combined with rock vibrato, pinch harmonics are a great way to accentuate notes in solos.

The pinch technique itself can be tricky to grasp initially, so be prepared for some trial and error before it clicks. In essence, pick the string with a downstroke aiming to push the pick *through* the string so that the outside edge of your thumb touches the string immediately after the pick does. It helps to leave only a small amount of the pick's tip protruding from your fingers.

As soon as the thumb has made contact with the string remove your hand, otherwise you will deaden the string completely.

Changing where you pick the string will change the pitch of the harmonic produced. Higher pitched harmonics will be found closer to the bridge pickup and lower pitched ones are created over the neck pickup. Experiment by moving your hand up and down the string between the bridge pickup and the neck.

**Fig. 2**

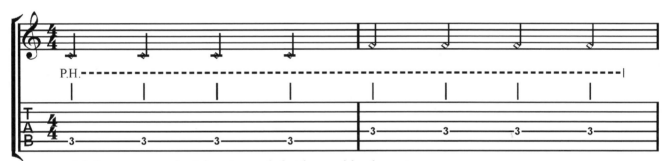

*pick from over neck pickup towards bridge and back again*

Our first pinch harmonic riff example is slow and heavy, allowing you plenty of space to focus on the pinch harmonics.

**Example 5e:**

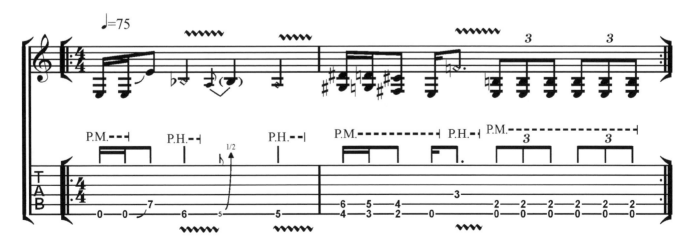

The bend in bar one should be slow and exaggerated and the palm muting should almost deaden the completely to get a very percussive sound. Accentuate the wide vibrato.

The next example is in the style of Slipknot's guitarists Mick Thompson and Jim Root and combines tight staccato rhythms with pinch harmonics.

Getting a strong vibrato on the harmonics really helps them to sing out. I chose to pick the first harmonic near to the bridge to create a higher pitch, and to pick the second harmonic over the neck pickup to produce a lower pitch.

**Example 5f:**

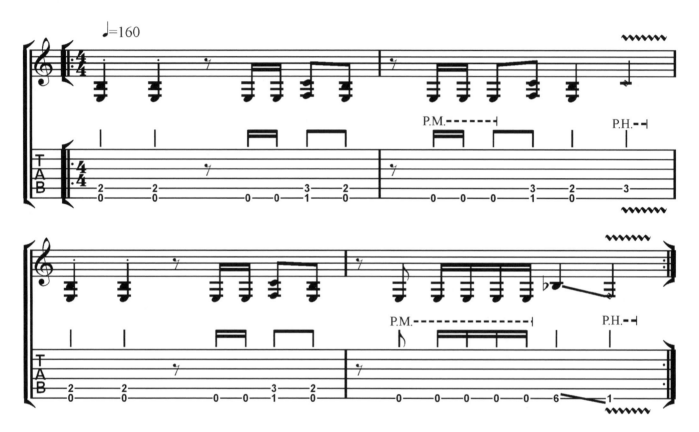

The above riff contrasts cropped low chugs with harmonics, so be sure to mute carefully with the fretting hand and keep the first few notes between each power chord detached.

The repeated harmonics in the following riff can be hard to nail, especially if pinched harmonics are new to you. The principle is similar to example 5d, but now we are using the thumb of the picking hand to touch the harmonic points instead of the fretting hand.

As you pick down through the string to catch the pinched harmonics, move the picking hand along the area from the bridge to the top of the fretboard to bring out different pitches. Revert back to normal picking for the power chords.

**Example 5g:**

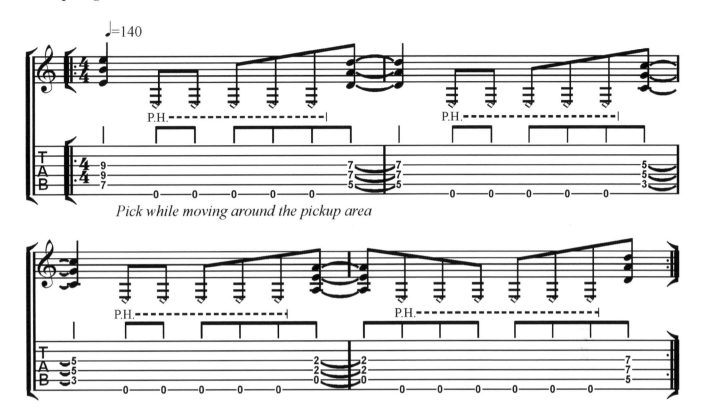

*Pick while moving around the pickup area*

The final example involves both hands and demonstrates how to move from alternate picking to pinch harmonics. Perfect the string crossing slowly, and keep the first finger of the fretting hand flattened to mute unused strings.

**Example 5h:**

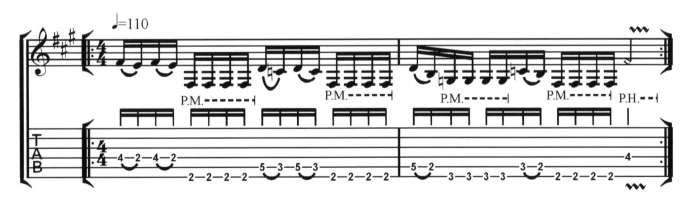

# Tapped Harmonics

Tapped harmonics are less common than the previous techniques but sound great when played with distortion. They are a fun way to decorate a note *after* it has been picked.

The idea is to play a note normally and then to quickly tap on the fret wire 12 frets above the fretted note. The tapped note is not held: instead you should aim to bounce off the string as quickly as possible.

Vibrato, bends and whammy can all be added after the harmonic is achieved. Try some tapped harmonics in isolation to start with. Remember the bracketed fret number in the tab corresponds to the tapped note and the previous note should still be held down.

**Fig. 3**

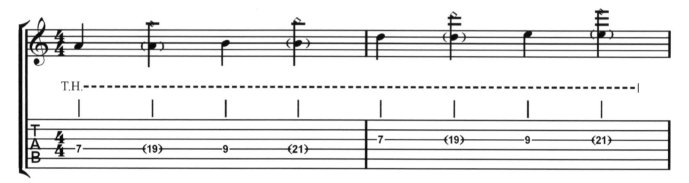

In example 5i, a 16th-note triplet rhythm is interspersed with tapped harmonics. Make the most of these harmonics and use a slow, wide vibrato. Good vibrato will enhance the 'scream' effect of the harmonic.

When changing between rhythm and lead ideas, be sure to quickly mute the unused strings. Generally, the palm of the picking hand should cover the bass strings when playing lead and the fretting hand fingers should lie across the treble strings when playing rhythm on the bass strings.

**Example 5i:**

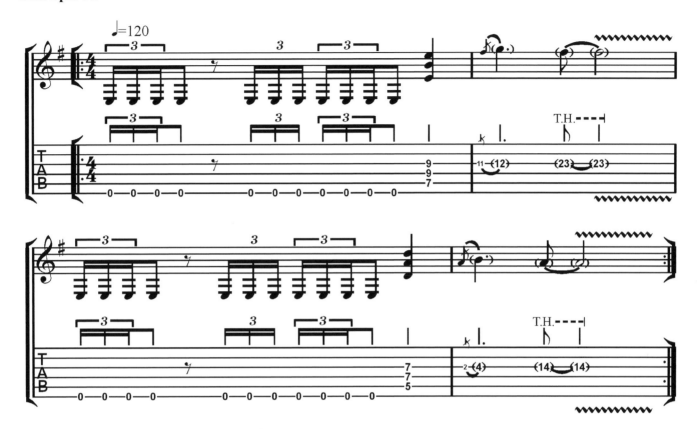

Example 5j shows how tapped harmonics can be used to embellish a sustaining chord as well as single notes.

The first four harmonics are tapped 12 frets above the fretted note. In the second shape, the tap is 7 frets higher than the fretted note producing harmonics an octave and a fifth higher.

**Example 5j:**

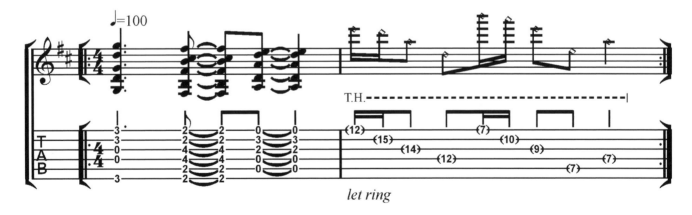

*let ring*

Note that the fret numbers in bar two of the tablature signify the frets that the *picking* hand should tap to create the harmonics, while the final Dsus2 chord remains held from the previous bar.

Dream Theater bassist, John Myung can be heard using harmonic ideas like this on *Images and Words* and *Awake,* and they work equally well on guitar. Moderate distortion will provide 'glisten' to the harmonics without turning them into poorly defined mush. Try rolling the volume pot on your guitar down to about seven to get less distortion from your amp.

Harmonics are a great way to widen your palette of sounds, but also think about their placement within the song when writing riffs. For example, a riff that is accompanying a strong vocal melody may not be the best place to let rip with squealing pitch harmonics. Likewise, a held chord under a keyboard or drum embellishment may be all that's needed and the addition of touch harmonics would clutter the texture. Knowing when to hold back will help make your writing more dynamic and effective.

**Songs that use Harmonics:**

The Dixie Dregs – *Take it Off the Top* (intro)

Ozzy Osbourne/Jake E. Lee – *Bark at the Moon* (half time bridge)

Megadeth – *Tornado of Souls* (intro)

Dream Theater – *Erotomania* (final intro reprise)

Pantera – *Cowboys from Hell* (post-solo riff)

Machinehead – *Imperium*

Black Label Society – *Suicide Messiah*

Slipknot – *Duality* (pre-verse/bridge)

Racer X – *Superheroes* (pre-chorus)

# Chapter Six: Riff Writing

So far we have looked at the many technical and theoretical aspects of playing metal guitar riffs. These should help you tackle your favourite songs and work on any technical challenges that arise.

My goal in writing this book was to help you develop the creativity and musical understanding to start writing new music. I want to continue now by focussing on the compositional aspect of metal guitar.

Once we have absorbed musical information (such as scales and technique) we must learn how to apply that knowledge and form a musical vocabulary. In this section of the book I'll be using the techniques and scales we've already looked at, but with an emphasis on using them creatively. I will examine how metal riffs are commonly constructed and look at some ideas you can use to get writing authentic sounding riffs yourself.

Most rock and metal riffs are built from a small melodic idea that is varied on repeating phrases. The purpose of a riff is to be a memorable, instrumental idea that energetically drives the song forward. Riffs can support vocal sections or instrumental solos where complex melodic ideas would be cluttered and distracting.

We will look at several compositional tools that are at your disposal such as pedal point, sequences and odd time signatures.

## Pedal Point Riffs

Pedal point is the technique of alternating a constant note with other notes or a changing melody. The pedal could also be held throughout as a drone while other notes move against it.

The term 'pedal point' originates from classical music, and is a reference to organ music where the lowest notes are played using the foot pedals rather than the keyboard. It is normal for the pedal note to be the bass note in the texture, but a high pedal is also possible, this is called an 'inverted' pedal.

There are plenty of classical motifs that are actually quite 'metal', and pedal point is definitely a common factor. Listen for pedal points in the intro to *Summer - Presto* from Vivaldi's Four Seasons and J.S. Bach's much loved Toccata and Fugue in D Minor (which were undoubtedly influences on neoclassical rock guitarists.)

Pedal tone riffs were particularly popular with the thrash metal bands of the '80s and our first example clearly illustrates the concept. In example 6a we alternate the notes of the A Natural Minor scale with the open A string.

Take care to keep the unused strings quiet throughout the exercise by gently dampening the higher strings with spare fingers.

Try to use down-picking throughout to get the best tone and attack.

**Example 6a:**

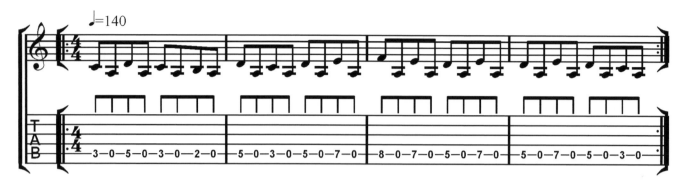

The next idea is similar, but the moving pitches are all on the off beats. Changing rhythmic emphasis can make a huge difference to how a riff feels to play. Master these first two examples so that you can comfortably place the fretted notes either on, or off the beat.

**Example 6b:**

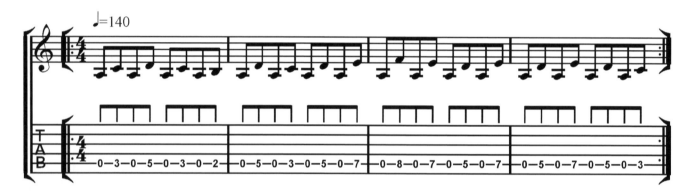

These riffs are also a great way to learn scales along the length of each string while also practicing picking control and stamina. Try playing different scales along the length of each string to create pedal point riffs.

In example 6c, we add extra open strings to the idea so that the fretted notes occur on a mixture of on and off beats. By creating less predictable rhythmic patterns for the melody, you can maintain the listeners' interest.

**Example 6c:**

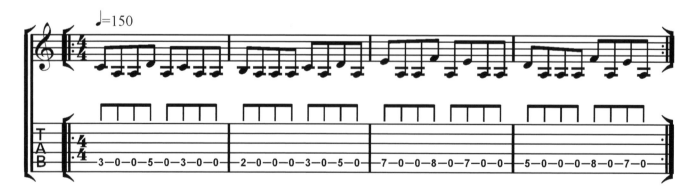

Try to create your own riffs in this style by varying the pitches and the rhythms.

The previous examples alternate between a single note and the pedal tone, but now we will alternate *two* notes with the pedal tone. Pay attention to the rhythmic phrasing here; the two fretted notes combined with one pedal note means that the pattern repeats every three notes. This creates what is known as a *cross-rhythm*.

Listen to the audio example to help you to feel the rhythm correctly.

**Example 6d:**

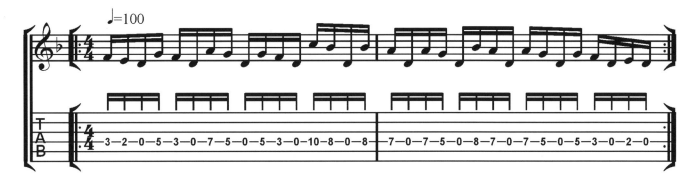

While the *motif* in the previous example was the moving part, the next example uses a pedal motif that alternates with a moving single note. This example is a great string crossing exercise to develop alternate picking, and will quickly help you to increase your accuracy and control.

**Example 6e:**

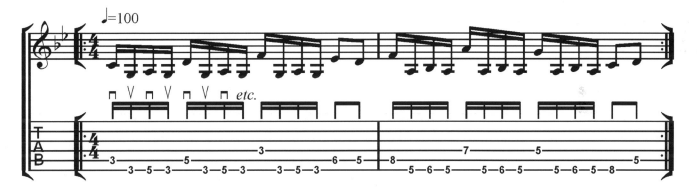

The pedal point in example 6f is combined with the reverse gallop rhythm. Be careful to synchronise your hands to ensure that the melody is heard clearly. Try to maintain an 1/8th note pulse of down-strokes, and use alternate picking for the 1/16th notes. **Example 6f:**

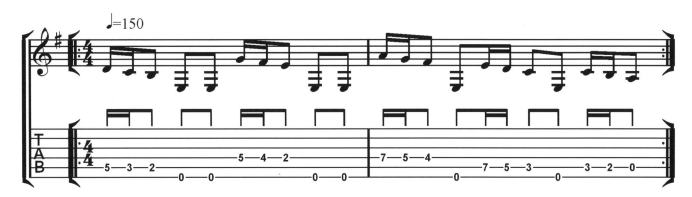

Most metal riffs are in 'open string' keys such as E and A, however, this next example is in the less common key of Eb minor.

The lack of open strings in this key makes riffing more difficult. The more complex fingering needed is a worthwhile challenge as it allows you to re-arrange existing songs and transpose ideas to different keys. To illustrate, example 6g is, in fact, example 6a transposed from E minor to Eb minor.

**Example 6g:**

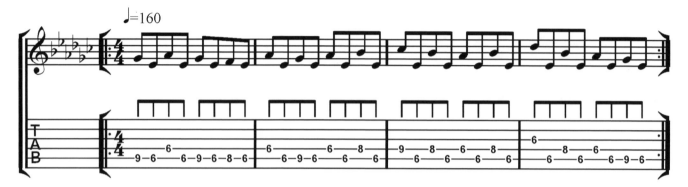

The following example requires relaxed alternate picking to play the fast 1/16th notes. Keeping the arc of the pick motion as small as possible will help to achieve the speed. It is common for this kind of idea to be played in unison with the double kick drum pattern so you must be rhythmically accurate to stay locked in time. The accenting technique discussed in chapter three will pay dividends here.

Accenting the fretted notes will help you to keep time. Using legato for the last two beats of bar two varies the tone of the riff and also gives the picking hand a brief rest to reduce the risk of cramping up.

**Example 6h:**

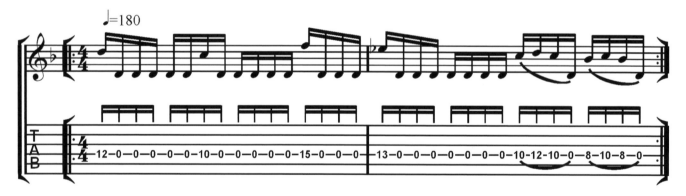

Example 6i is another death metal riff using an open E pedal tone against a short chromatic motif. Again, try to accent the motif with the picking hand once you have developed enough control to play it accurately. Accenting certain notes brings riffs to life by adding a sense of light and shade.

**Example 6i:**

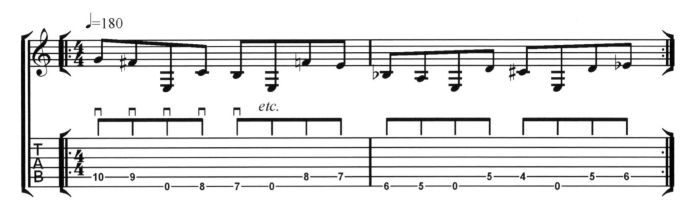

**Riffs that feature pedal point:**

Iron Maiden – *Wasted Years*

Ozzy Osbourne – *Crazy Train* (verse)

Metallica – *Damage Inc.* (bridge)

Yngwie Malmsteen – *Vengeance*

Dream Theater – *Panic Attack* (intro)

Muse – *Stockholm Syndrome*

Arch Enemy – *Nemesis*

# Sequencing Riffs

Music with the most powerful impact strikes a balance between unity and variety. In other words, it should be able to hold the audience's interest by developing in new way, while still relating to what has already been heard. Sequences are a great way to achieve this kind of structure and are a popular device in all styles of music.

Baroque harpsichord music was full of sequences, and this proved to be a great influence on rock soloing in the '70s and '80s. If this interests you, I can recommend the inventions of J.S. Bach, and sonatas of Scarlatti to improve your understanding of scale patterns.

The following simple rock riff uses the A minor pentatonic scale. The triplet feel synchronises with the descending sequence of three notes. If you use legato, be careful to get the timing as precise as if you were picking.

**Example 7a:**

Our second example uses a pattern of three notes in B natural minor but now the example is played with a straight feel. This means that the start of each group of three falls on a different part of the beat each time to create a commonly used cross-rhythm.

If you take some time to internalise the rhythm, you will start to feel both the three-note groupings and the 1/4 note pulse simultaneously. Accent the first note of each three-note motif and tap your foot on the 1/4 note pulse.

**Example 7b:**

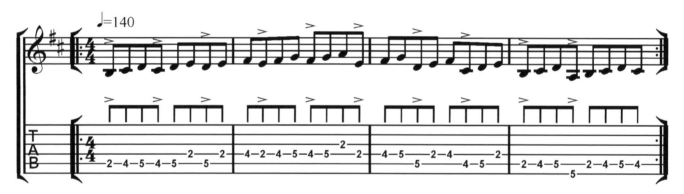

Now try mixing fragments of this scale sequence with picking cells on an open string pedal note. Notice how the timing of the riff becomes syncopated by varying the length of each sequence pattern. Take your time to get the rhythm memorised accurately before speeding up.

**Example 7c:**

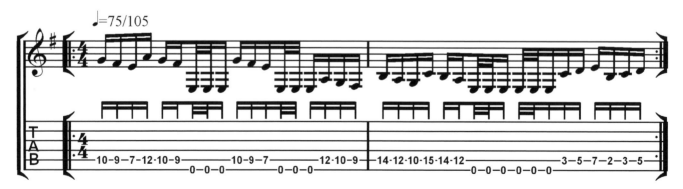

In example 7d, a two-bar pedal point idea is sequenced through several steps of the C# minor scale. Although the chord symbols show power chords, the double-stops in the riff change to accommodate the expected major or minor tonality of each pedal note.

Consistent down-picking would normally be used to play this idea, but you may like to try using hybrid picking. Plucking the high double stops with the middle and ring fingers together helps them to jump out with more twang and attack.

**Example 7d:**

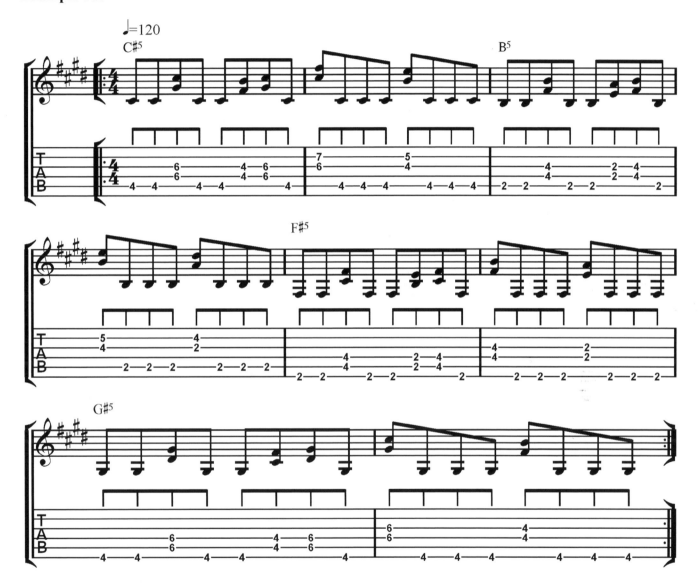

Example 7e is a long phrase in E Phrygian that moves through different positions on the neck. The initial phrase is adapted to fit the notes of the scale in each shape.

**Example 7e:**

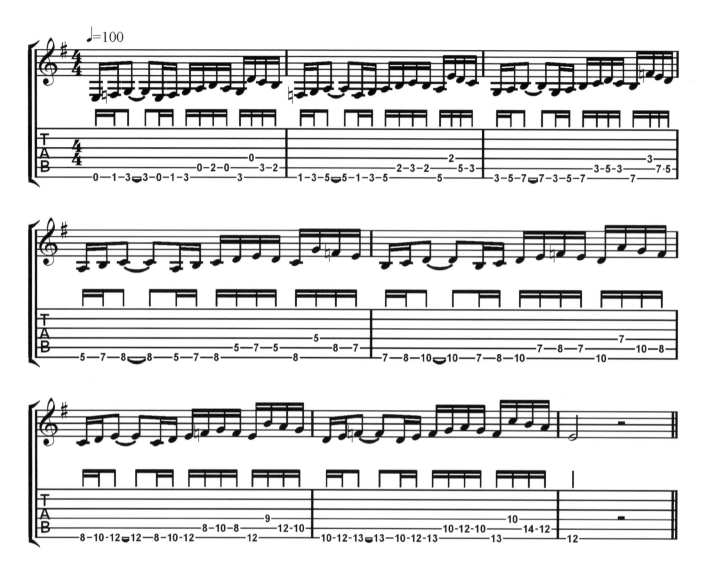

This idea could be played by moving across the strings in one position, but there are three main advantages to shifting it along the neck.

- It is easier to visualise for the fretting hand

- The picking part remains the same for every iteration in the sequence

- The tone of the notes remains more consistent

Always try to play on the lowest strings of the guitar when a thick rock tone is desired because they provide more bass and midrange frequencies.

It is possible to create interesting rhythmic variations by applying mathematical rules to the development of a musical idea. Example 7f contains an idea characteristic of progressive metal bands like Dream Theater and Spastic Ink.

There are two sequences at work in the following example. Firstly, the melodic notes move up through the E Aeolian scale with each repetition of the phrase. Secondly, we gradually truncate our original four-beat pattern, so the repetitions get shorter in length.

In bar three, the final four notes of the original riff are discarded. Two bars later, the first four notes of the pattern are removed, and again at bar seven another four notes are lost, leaving the final two repetitions containing only four notes from the original sixteen. Count carefully to avoid getting lost.

**Example 7f:**

This gradual shortening of the pattern delivers a sense of speeding up, although the tempo does not change. The effect of this developing musical idea is to build to a strong climax after the tension of the rhythmic and melodic sequences.

The next example develops the idea of 'subtractive' rhythmic sequences. This time we have a scale pattern that lasts for eight 1/16th notes. Every time the phrase repeats we lose a note until only one is left. The process then reverses and adds one note at a time to grow again to the original motif.

To help with timing and control use alternate picking, but be aware that the phrase will sometimes start on a down-stroke and sometimes on an upstroke because of the changing phrase lengths. It is good to practice phrases starting on both an upstroke and a downstroke to prepare you for these uneven types of riffs.

**Example 7g:**

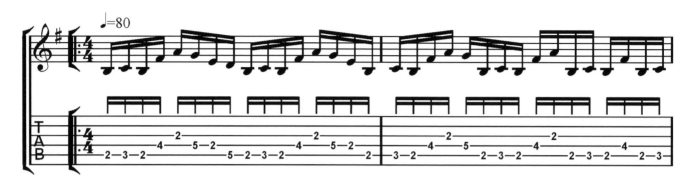

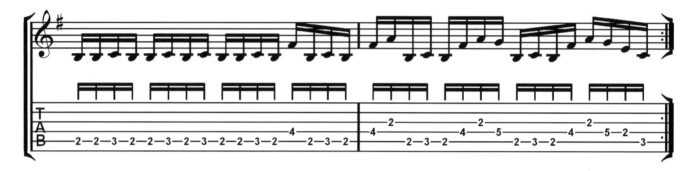

The piece *Coming Together* by contemporary American composer Frederic Rzewski is a great example of this kind of pattern based writing

**Riffs that Contain Sequencing:**

Racer X – *Technical Difficulties*

Nevermore – *Born*

Lovefist – *Dangerous B\*stard* (bridge riff)

Black Sabbath – *Symphony of the Universe*

Pantera – *Cowboys from Hell*

Dream Theater – *Fatal Tragedy* (structure of guitar/keys solos)

Angra – *Speed*

# Odd Time Signatures

The last few examples delved briefly into the world of odd time signatures, but so far nearly all of the examples in the book have been written in 4/4. The vast majority of music you have ever heard is written in 4/4, which is why it sounds so natural. However, depending on your cultural heritage, other metres like 5/4, 7/4 or 7/8 may also feel completely natural and easy to dance to.

Odd time signatures are particularly common in traditional Balkan and North African music.

Many metal bands, particularly those influenced by world music or progressive rock, have used odd time signatures for entire songs without any unbalancing effect (for example Tool's *Jambi*, or Alice in Chains' *Them Bones*), although odd time signatures normally do create a sense of musical tension.

Just as dissonant harmony creates a tension that needs to resolve, uneven rhythmic phrasing also creates a 'metric dissonance' that is resolved by moving to an even time signature.

The key to playing in any time signature (and developing a strong sense of time in general) is learning to feel the rhythm of the music instinctively. Counting out loud is a good start, but repetition and listening to a lot of music in different metres are both vital if you are to master odd time.

Let's recap how rhythms can be divided so as to help understand how odd time signatures are phrased and felt.

As you know, a bar of 4/4 is divided equally into four 1/4 notes. Each 1/4 note is divided into two 1/8th notes and these can be further divided into 1/16th notes:

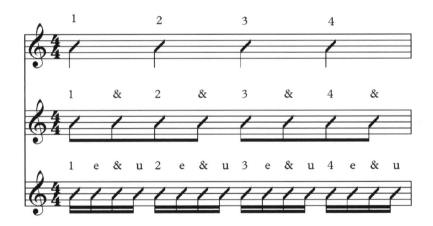

A bar of 6/8 is divided into six 1/8th notes with the accents on the first and fourth 1/8th note. Although a bar of 6/8 is the same length as a bar of 3/4, 6/8 feels like two groups of triplets. 3/4 feels like a single, slower group of three.

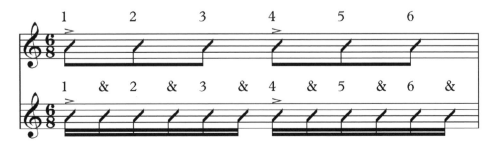

Learning to feel combinations of triple and even times opens a new rhythmic vocabulary. This kind of feel is common to the traditional music of several Balkan countries, and in the work of 20th Century classical composers like Bartok and Stravinsky, who were inspired by the music of other cultures. In fact, many metal musicians cite Stravinsky as an inspiration, so check out a recording of his bombastic orchestral masterpiece 'The Rite of Spring' – it's pure metal!

To begin our look at odd time signatures, we will start with 6/8. Though not an 'odd' time signature, 6/8 is less common than 4/4, and exploring its possibilities will help you get to grips with other, more complex meters.

Tap your foot on the first and fourth beats of the bar. Listen to the click in the audio to help you feel the three note phrasing.

**Example 8a:**

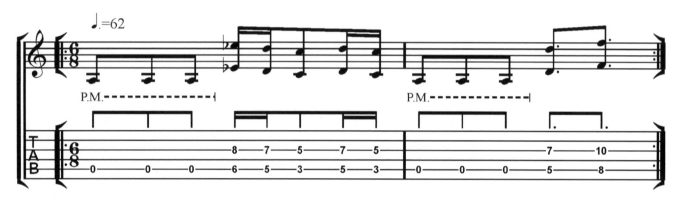

If you find yourself struggling, tap your foot on all six 1/8th note beats to help you internalise the subdivisions and become comfortable with the rhythm.

The next example highlights the subtle difference between 6/8 and 3/4. A classic example of this rhythm is *America* from Leonard Bernstein's *West Side Story*, later covered by early progressive rock group The Nice.

Keeping those lyrics in mind will help you connect to the shifting pulse of the music.

## Example 8b:

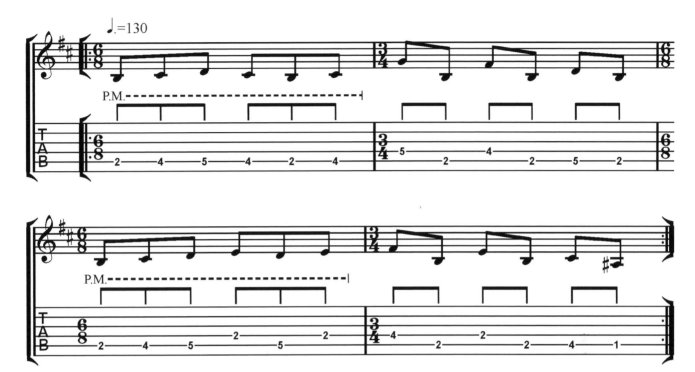

This next riff in 7/4 features many sliding power chords. Very often there are different ways of notating a musical idea that subtly change where the rhythmic emphasis lies. This riff could also have been notated as alternating bars of 4/4 and 3/4.

## Example 8c:

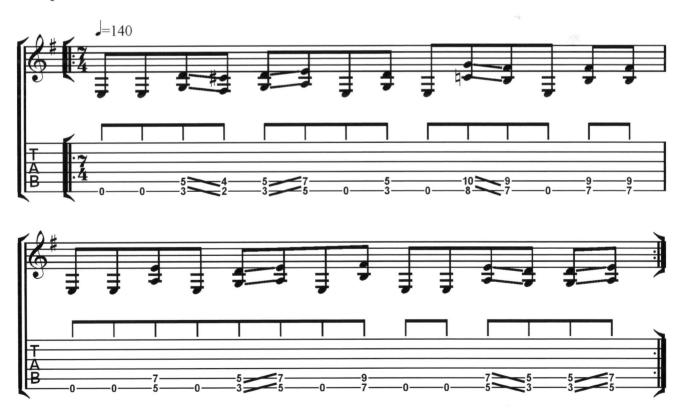

## 1/8th Note Odd Time Signatures

7/8 is half the length of 7/4 and can be felt like a bar of 4/4 with the last 1/8 note removed to leave three and a half beats per bar. The effect is that the pulse now feels rushed as beat one comes earlier than expected and this sense of instability builds rhythmic tension.

**Example 8d:**

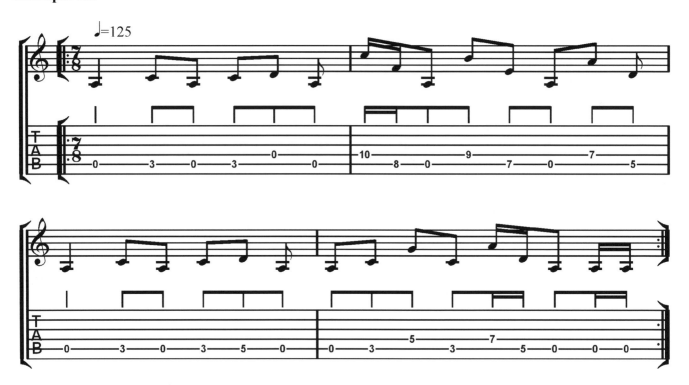

7/8 can be heard in the intro to Steve Vai's *The Attitude Song*.

The time signature of 5/8 can be felt like 6/8 with the final 1/8th note removed. Compare example 8e with example 8a and you will see that the phrasing is similar.

To feel 5/8, count to five while accenting beats one and four. Once you have begun to internalise the sound and feel of the following riff, you can stop counting and it should feel like one long beat followed by a shorter one.

**Example 8e:**

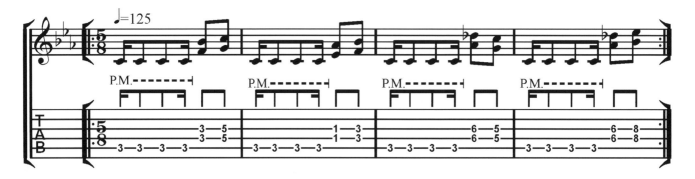

5/8 can be heard in the middle section of Dream Theater's *Octavarium*.

## Combining Time Signatures

Just as we varied melodic motifs by transposing them to different pitches in the sequencing chapter, we can vary the time signatures of riffs by adding or subtracting notes.

In this example, both bars are essentially the same but an 1/8th note is added to the end of the second bar.

**Example 8f:**

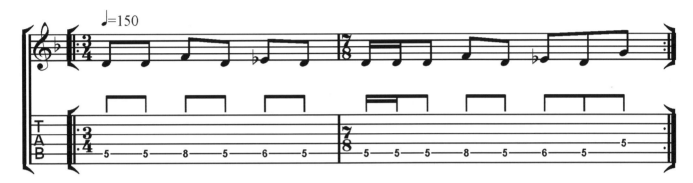

A similar example of this 'additive' process is heard in the bridge section of Mastodon's *Blood & Thunder*.

Another example of the same concept begins with a bar of 4/4, but this time we *subtract* an 1/8th note and create a bar of 7/8. The first bar is then repeated and answered by a bar of 9/8 (this time *adding* one 1/8th note).

**Example 8g:**

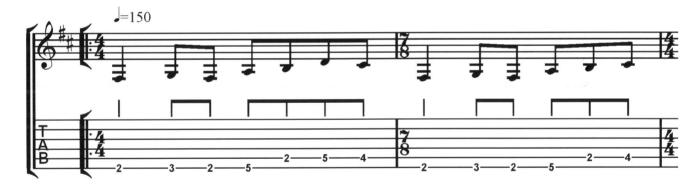

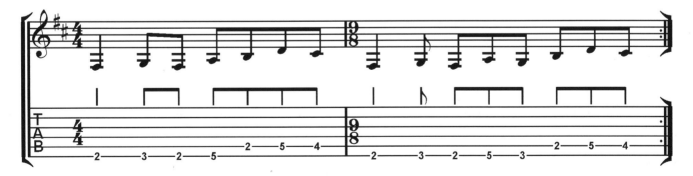

This type of metric variation is found in the intro to the Symphony X song *Inferno*.

Odd time signatures can be mathematically confusing, so when writing riffs it is often more creative to play the idea as you hear it, and figure out the time signatures later.

Next we combine both pitch *and* metric variation. This is a common idea in progressive rock, metal and fusion. Work through each bar carefully and memorise it in isolation. It can be easy to lose your place, especially when you are new to these kinds of ideas. Try clapping along with the audio to internalise the pulse.

**Example 8h:**

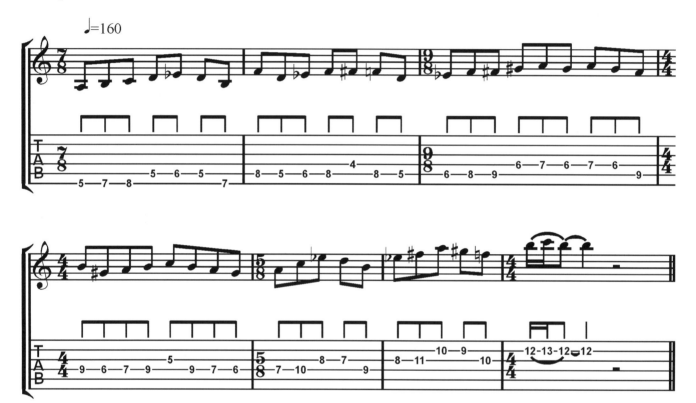

Use consistent alternate picking to play this example, but be aware that some bars will start on an upstroke because of the odd bar lengths. Accentuate the start of each bar with a harder pick stroke, even if it is an upstroke.

## 1/16th Note Odd Time Signatures

While 5/8 and 7/8 were based around 1/8th note divisions, the following time signatures divide the beat at a 1/16th note level. 1/16th note time signatures can look intimidating on paper, but the principle of subdividing the beats remains the same.

The next example is written in 11/16 which is formed from two 1/4 note beats and three 1/16th notes. To follow along to the audio you should count the 1/16th notes. Counting in 11/16 can be difficult at faster speeds, but the following figure shows how to count through the bar.

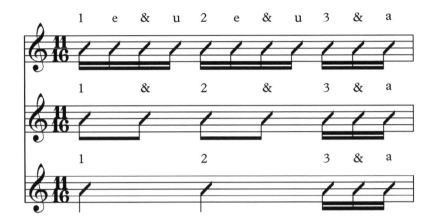

**Example 8i:**

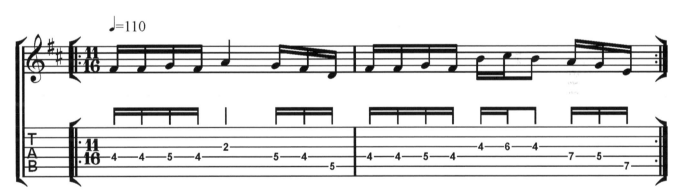

The next idea is written in 15/16. A good way to practice these riffs is to slow them down and tap your foot in 1/8th notes to provide more reference points.

Try splitting the bar of 15/16 up into smaller portions to make things more manageable. For example, the first two 1/4 note beats can be practiced separately from the remaining seven semiquavers. (The feel of seven should be familiar from the examples in 7/8).

Pieces the second bar together in a similar fashion, and when all the parts are comfortably under the fingers, combine the two bars to form the full riff.

**Example 8j:**

These 1/16th note based time signatures occur in the music of bands like Planet X and Sikth and can be disorientating at first, but that is often the intended musical effect!

Odd time signatures could fill a whole book by themselves and the possibilities of combining and layering them is almost infinite. However, this chapter should have helped you start to recognise them when listening to music, and understand how they can be broken down logically.

**Songs that feature odd time signatures:**

Tool – *Vicarious* (5/4)

Metallica – *Blackened* (7/4, 3/4)

Dream Theater – *The Test That Stumped Them All* (7/8)

Mastodon – *The Wolf Is Loose* (7/8)

Machinehead – *Days Turn Blue to Grey* (7/8)

Cynic – *Textures* (9/8)

Pantera – *I'm Broken* (7/8)

Slipknot – *Welcome* (10/8)

Planet X – *Snuff (5/4, 7/8, 11/16)*

Gojira – *The Art of Dying* (21/16)

# Chapter Seven: Drop D Tuning

Up until now every example has been played in 'standard' EADGBE tuning, however, it is common for metal guitarists to use a number of other tunings. Using different tuning offers new musical possibilities and they can help to break out of creative ruts by forcing you to abandon tired patterns and fingerings.

Most alternate tunings in metal lower the pitch of the strings to create a heavier sound, but they can also be used to transpose open-string riffs to a key that is more comfortable for the singer.

As a string's pitch is lowered, the string will become floppy due to the lack of tension making accurate picking more challenging and possibly resulting in a poorly defined attack. If you intend to use a lower tuning for a prolonged period, switch to a heavier gauge of strings. Many string manufacturers produce sets designed for down tuning.

Alternate tunings is a very broad topic, and the range of tunings available could fill a whole book. In this chapter, we'll look at how metal guitarists use the most common alternative tuning, *Drop D*.

Most alternate tunings in metal are transposed forms of either standard or drop D tuning. This means that the intervals between the strings will remain the same while the tuning of whole guitar is shifted down. For this reason, most players will still be thinking in terms of standard tuning, no matter what pitch they've actually tuned to.

Drop D was particularly popular with the nu-metal and alternative rock groups of the '90s and early 2000s to create thick power-chord based riffs.

Drop D tuning lowers the low E string by a whole step to D so that the interval between the lowest two strings is now a fifth. This means that power chords can be played easily by simply barring across the bottom three strings. Power chords riffs that might otherwise be too difficult to execute cleanly are now easily achievable. Check out the middle section of Slipknot's *Surfacing*, where a fast chromatic single note riff is repeated as power chords using Drop D tuning.

In example 9a, play the power chords in the example using either the first or third finger of the fretting hand as if you were playing a single note, but flatten the finger down across three strings. Experiment with finger angle and pressure so that you keep the higher strings silent by muting with the underside of the fingers.

**Example 9a:**

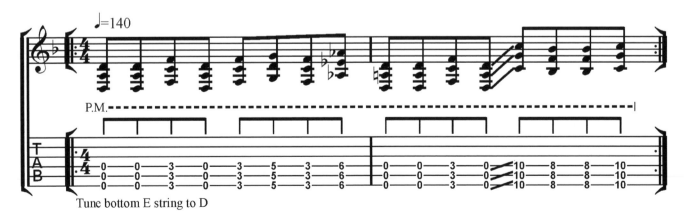

Tune bottom E string to D

These kind of grinding Drop D riffs combined with a disco influenced drum beat helped create Rammstein's distinctive sound.

Having the low E string tuned down a whole step changes how its notes relate to the notes on the other strings. In Drop D tuning, the higher octave D is now located at the fifth fret of the A string, whereas in standard E tuning, the octave E is located at the seventh fret. Metal players in Drop D tuning make great use of this octave jump, so know its location is very important. This idea is shown in the following example.

**Example 9b:**

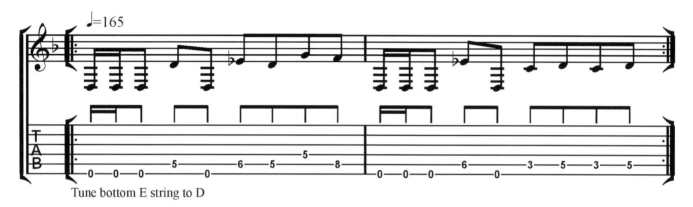

Tune bottom E string to D

The following example uses Drop D tuning to play in E minor. This riff would be impossible in standard tuning because of the use of the b7 (D) below the root.

**Example 9c:**

Tune bottom E string to D

In Drop D tuning, both the sixth and fourth strings are tuned to the note D, which lets us play with some cool new ideas. Here's a pedal point riff on the 4th string, repeated on the 6th string.

Watch out for the 5/4 time of this example. Listen to the audio to get the rhythm firmly in your head.

**Example 9d:**

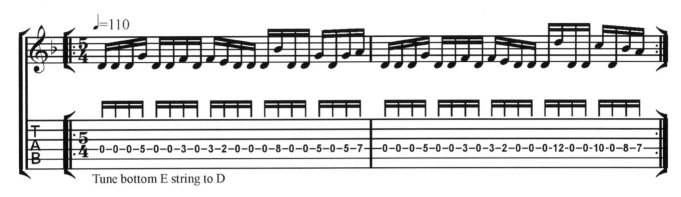

Tune bottom E string to D

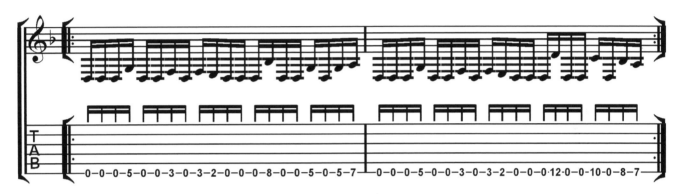

The first line of this riff could form an effective intro to a song, starting out with a single guitar playing the line on the higher D string before the whole band joins in and the riff jumps down an octave to the low D string. Thanks to the Drop D tuning, the riff can easily drop an octave while the fingering remains the same.

Experimenting with other tunings that break up the standard tuning intervals can produce great and unexpected ideas. Try detuning one or two strings by a tone and playing normal chord shapes to hear what happens! Let your ear guide you in deciding whether you like the results. You can always figure out the names of your new chords or scales later.

The use of seven- and eight-string guitars is becoming increasingly common among technical and progressive metal guitarists, having been first popularised by Steve Vai and nu-metallers KoRn in the '90s. These instruments allow access to lower pitches without sacrificing the normal note range of standard tuning. They can also create interesting chordal opportunities by moving bass notes up the neck.

**Bands that use Alternative Tunings:**

Rammstein – Drop D

Killswitch Engage – Drop C (CGCFAD)

Between the Buried and Me – C# standard (C#F#BEG#C#)

Slipknot – Drop B (BF#BEG#C#)

KoRn – 7 string guitars, Drop A (ADGCFAD)

Black Label Society (BADGBE on *Low Down*)

# Chapter Eight: Getting a Great Sound

After examining so many elements of metal guitar, we should talk about how to get the best sound when we play. The wide range of guitars, amps, pedals and pickups on the market can make finding the right gear a long and potentially expensive process. In this chapter, I'll discuss gear and effects to help you to make informed choices when buying equipment.

I've also included some pointers to help you get the best tone out of your fingers and equipment.

Guitarists often find that when they first play with a band after practicing alone, their sound is not as they would like. Often, the guitar seems too quiet or too mushy and thin. The most common cause for this is too much distortion and destructive EQ settings, although it's often blamed on the amp being too small or a need for different pedals.

While good quality gear helps to create a professional sound, it is also easy to create a bad sound on a top-of-the-range amplifier. Knowing *how* to set an amplifier is a big factor. The most important thing to understand is that a great, low volume tone in your bedroom will sound very different on stage or in the rehearsal room.

Thankfully all amplifiers work on the same principles, so by learning how to use the features on one amp you will understand what to expect from the others that you will come across in future.

## Equalisation (EQ)

EQ is the most important tool for altering the tone of your guitar, and everything from your guitar's tone pot to your wah-wah pedal is a form of EQ because they all filter the frequency of the guitar in some way. Some of the most important changes to your tone however, are created by the equalisation controls on your amplifier.

Whether your amp has simple controls for bass, middle and treble or a full multi-band graphic EQ, the amp's tone controls separate the guitar's sound into separate tonal 'bands' allowing you to independently alter the relative volumes of each band.

One common misuse of EQ is to 'scoop the mids' by turning down the mid EQ tone control on the amp. This sound has been often emulated since it was heard on early thrash recordings. The problem is that while this scooped tone works great in the bedroom (or even on recordings where the guitar has been tracked on its own), these middle frequencies form the main body of the guitar's sound. Cutting the mids can cause the guitar to disappear entirely when played alongside bass and drums. This issue is exacerbated by lower priced beginner amps having less pronounced mid frequencies to begin with.

If you're not cutting through in the mix try boosting the middle frequencies on your amp to create a more prominent rhythm tone. Rock guitarists often use an external EQ pedal to further boost their mid-range which helps solos cut through the mix.

# Valve or Solid-State?

Traditional valve amps use vacuum tubes to amplify your guitar's signal. They are typically more expensive and considerably heavier than transistor amps. Valve amps are characterised by warmer, more pronounced midrange frequencies. The tone of a valve amp changes as its volume increases because the valves compress the guitar signal to produce a type of distortion known as *overdrive* when they are worked harder.

Although a rich, valve-generated distortion is very desirable, having to find different settings depending on the volume can be irritating.

In contrast, solid-state or *transistor* amplifiers, are usually cheaper, lighter and more robust than valve amps so they are better suited to the wear and tear of gigging.

The distortion and overdrive channels on a solid state amp may sound harsher and more brittle than a valve amp. However, there are guitarists who have favoured this sound, most notably Dimebag Darrel in the Pantera years.

It can be tempting to buy large, impressive looking amps, especially if it is the model a favourite guitarist uses. However, the nature of valve amplification normally means that a big amp used at a low volume delivers a less desirable tone than a small amp that is working hard. Be realistic! If you're playing in your bedroom, do you really need a 100-watt stack?! A 15-watt, all-valve amplifier can more than handle the average bar gig.

# Amplifier vs. Rack/Amp modelling?

In recent years, the quality of multi-fx and amp modelling hardware has developed rapidly. Whether through laptop software, pedals or dedicated rack units, you can quickly replicate the sound of whatever amp you desire at a fraction of the cost of acquiring the original. This is a tempting option, especially for guitarists who want to create a diverse range of tones.

Modelling devices often work on a *patch* based system, meaning that all the parameters of a sound (amp type, settings, booster, effects, signal chain etc) can be changed simultaneously with just one button, rather than tap-dancing across a whole pedal board mid-song.

The trade-off to this flexibility is that the sound produced is still an emulation of 'real' gear, and only the very best amplifier modelling equipment responds well to dynamic changes in your playing. If you can achieve the range of sounds you need with just the channels on the amp and a modest number of pedals, then it could be better to invest in one quality amplifier rather than a multi-fx or modelling amp.

# Boosts, Distortion and Noise gates

Unlike a distortion pedal which adds 'artificial' distortion to the guitar, a boost pedal simply makes the input signal to the amp louder so the amp's tubes will provide more compression and natural distortion.

Many players will use a boost pedal in conjunction with their amp's overdrive to create their rhythm tone. A secondary boost pedal is often used to raise the signal and add gain when soloing. The most popular boost pedal is the Ibanez Tubescreamer, whose name nicely describes the pedal's purpose.

When you increase the level of gain on a signal there is likely to be an increase in the electronic noise created along the signal path resulting in a hum or buzz through the amp. This hum can be especially problematic when playing loudly at gigs or band rehearsals. This hum is avoided by using a *noise gate*.

Noise gates set a *threshold* volume for the signal. The noise gate closes when the input signal from the guitar drops below the threshold and stops all signal passing through, including any buzz from the pedals. When you start playing, the signal will exceed the set threshold and the gate will open allowing all sound through, however the hum is now lost under the guitar signal.

## Tone is in the Fingers

Great guitarists are as identifiable by their 'sound' as by the actual notes that they play. Owning all of your favourite player's equipment often won't make you sound at all like them because tone is as much about touch and articulation as it is about guitar and amp choice.

It makes sense to develop a great touch on the instrument before considering how you will then process the signal with effects or the amp. The idea is to enhance a strong tone, rather than have to make up for inadequacies in your playing.

Practicing unplugged or through a clean amp is often very revealing because distortion can mask a multitude of sins. Experiment by varying the angle of the pick, and where on the strings you are playing to find different tones. Picking close to the bridge will give more treble while picking over the fretboard will accentuate the bass and mid-range frequencies.

An electric guitar can be adjusted at the bridge, saddles and truss rod to make the guitar feel as comfortable to play as possible. A good setup can often transform an inexpensive guitar into a very playable one.

The distance between the strings and the fretboard is known as the *action* and the action is mainly adjusted on the bridge of the guitar. A low action will feel easier to play as it requires less energy and movement to fret, but there is often a loss of tone.

Try to keep the action as high as possible while still being able to execute your ideas perfectly and not having to work too hard. Since the '80s, the norm is for metal guitarists to play with very low actions (to the point of the strings almost buzzing against the frets), but the tone of these players can sometimes be lacklustre when it comes to sustaining long notes.

## Strings and Picks

A small change in strings or picks can have a radical effect on the tone and the feel of your guitar. Thicker strings produce a beefier tone because there is more metal vibrating over the pickups, and because the strings are held at a higher tension.

The trade-off with thick strings is that they take more strength to bend so wide bends may prove difficult. As rock guitarists are usually expected to play both rhythm and lead parts, you may find it best to compromise by trying .10 gauge strings, as these are only slightly thicker than average. If you play rhythm guitar exclusively then you could consider something thicker for a beefier tone.

High tension on the strings can help with picking consistency at faster speeds. Heavy strings are quicker to react to a pick stroke whereas thin strings vibrate in a wider arc and produce a less defined tone.

The same logic also applies to picks: a more rigid pick will not be bent by the string and will produce a quicker, more consistent attack. Choosing a pick with a sharp (rather than a rounded) tip can also help to create a well-defined attack.

Many rock guitarists known for their picking prowess use picks that are at least 2mm thick, although there are always exceptions to the rule: Yngwie Malmsteen uses light gauge strings with thin picks and clearly has no issues with speed or consistency!

# Closing Words

Phew, there we have it! That concludes our tour of metal rhythm guitar. Though we've only scratched the surface of a hugely diverse genre of music I've tried to create a guide that encourages further learning and listening. With the skills gained by studying these pages, you should now be able to learn songs by yourself and apply these techniques in different situations.

As parting advice, I would say that the key to being a competent musician is to work evenly on the skills that combine to make you a well-rounded player.

Technical proficiency, aural awareness, theory, and playing with other musicians should all be practiced equally because each element supports the development of the others. There are many transcription books available, plus 'learn to play' DVDs and YouTube lessons that will spoon feed you information. However overdependence on these sources can mean that your ears remain underdeveloped. Make time to transcribe songs by ear too.

Transcribing riffs from records will connect the placement of notes on the neck to their sound. The ultimate goal is to be able to play something as soon as you hear it.

A strong ability to aurally interpret music will increase your pleasure both as a musician and as a listener. The tuition of foreign languages never neglects listening practice in the way that music tuition often seems to!

When you're listening to music, try to focus on the rhythm guitar parts and identify how the part is being played. Is it muted? Does it involve fast picking or are there hammer-ons and pull-offs?

Progress with aural skills is harder to measure than metronome speed or theoretical information, but every time you actively listen to music, transcribe, and sing melodies, you are training your ears. Every piece of experience will accumulate to make you a more aurally aware musician.

Thank you for reading this book, I hope it is helpful on your journey into metal guitar playing.

Rock on!

Rob

# Other Books from Fundamental Changes

*Heavy Metal Lead Guitar*

*Fretboard Fluency For Guitar*

*The Complete Guide to Playing Blues Guitar Book One: Rhythm Guitar*

*The Complete Guide to Playing Blues Guitar Book Two: Melodic Phrasing*

*The Complete Guide to Playing Blues Guitar Book Three: Beyond Pentatonics*

*The Complete Guide to Playing Blues Guitar Compilation*

*The CAGED System and 100 Licks for Blues Guitar*

*Fundamental Changes in Jazz Guitar: The Major ii V I*

*Minor ii V Mastery for Jazz Guitar*

*Chord Tone Soloing for Jazz Guitar*

*Jazz Blues Soloing for Guitar*

*Guitar Scales in Context*

*Guitar Chords in Context Part One*

*Jazz Guitar Chord Mastery (Guitar Chords in Context Part Two)*

*Complete Technique for Modern Guitar*

*Funk Guitar Mastery*

*The Complete Technique, Theory and Scales Compilation for Guitar*

*Sight Reading Mastery for Guitar*

*Rock Guitar Un-CAGED: The CAGED System and 100 Licks for Rock Guitar*

*The Practical Guide to Modern Music Theory for Guitarists*

*Beginner's Guitar Lessons: The Essential Guide*

## Be Social

For hundreds of free guitar lessons, check out **www.fundamental-changes.com**

**www.facebook.com/FundamentalChangesInGuitar**

**@RobThorpeMusic**

**@Guitar_Joseph**

37370768R00054

Made in the USA
Middletown, DE
01 December 2016